The Six

Dimensions

OF

C.H.A.N.G.E.

A Simple Guide to Getting What You Want

Kenny Chapman

The Six Dimensions of C.H.A.N.G.E.
A Simple Guide to Getting What You Want

Kenny Chapman

Copyright © 2009 by Kenny Chapman

Contact:
Kenny Chapman
570 S. Westgate Dr.
Grand Junction, CO 81505
877-YOUACHIEVE (877-968-2244)
www.kennychapman.net

Printed in the United States of America
Cover design/inside layout: TheBookProducer.com

ISBN: 978-0-9842017-0-9

This book is dedicated to my Mom,
who gave me life, hope, and the desire as a child
to become more than I ever dreamed possible.
Thank you Mom, I love you.

ACKNOWLEDGMENTS

I am deeply thankful for the loving support of my wife Christy. She is an integral part of helping me tap into the best within myself as I continue to share my message with the world. As a goal-oriented person I'm always moving in many directions at the same time, and she is always there for me.

I'm also very thankful for Seth Czerepak's diligent work in helping me bring this project to reality. Seth played a vital role in helping me share *The Six Dimensions of Change* with the world.

I have tremendous gratitude for the people in my life that gave me the space to make this book come to life. John Burwell, Jr., Robin Stevens, Sonja Cook, and Doug Hatter all worked together to take care of daily business while I was pursuing my goal of finishing this book.

Finally, I express great love and gratitude to my mother Jane, and late father, Ron, as without them this book would not exist. My friend Marcus Straub for always telling me the truth and helping me connect with my true self. My spiritual teachers, and of course the greatest teacher of all, my life.

TABLE OF CONTENTS

FOREWORD

Friends are great assets in your life. A friend will assist you with a task – not for payment – but as a gesture of love. You are about to discover a true friend in Kenny Chapman, and his book *The Six Dimensions of Change* is a gesture of love.

When you're looking for a car, it's nice to have a friend in the car business. If you are buying a diamond, having a friend in the diamond business will give you peace of mind. Reading Kenny's book give's you the experience that you have a friend helping you with your personal growth.

The strategies Kenny shares are the very steps he himself took to manifest his own dreams. Even if you yourself have goals that seem like attaining the moon, this book shows you that it doesn't take rocket science to get there. As you read, you will feel a quickening in your heart… because Kenny makes the process of realizing your goals seem logical – even easy.

For example, *The Six Dimensions of Change* reveals Truth in a way that makes you understand that you've known this all your life. How come you only see it NOW? That's Kenny's gift. He reminds you of things you already know, but have forgotten.

Because the book's contents seem so familiar, it is easy to read. You can open to any random page and find something that is relevant to your life *right now*!

The Six Dimensions of Change offers simple tools that will transform you. It contains many elements of a workbook; so rather than merely providing you with good ideas, Kenny involves you in a self-development workshop designed to bring you exactly what you've been seeking. His personal, friendly way of speaking makes you feel as if your next-door neighbor is using his own life to teach you something valuable and profound. Every point he makes is supported with clear, concise examples.

Kenny Chapman can be your Peak Performance Coach – a Personal Trainer for your future. Kenny's methods are guaranteed to work… if *you* do. Regardless of where you are on your path toward crystallizing your goals, Kenny constantly shines a light on pitfalls you might not have noticed – like self-defeating behaviors or a failure to pay attention. As you digest *The Six Dimensions of Change*, you will start knowing yourself a lot better. You will find the missing pieces to the puzzle of your life.

I enjoyed reading it.

Tolly Burkan,
author of *Let It Be Easy*

INTRODUCTION

Let's Get Ready

Before we get started, I want to thank you for giving me the opportunity to share the strategies I've used to turn my dreams into reality. I have a profound respect for anyone who has made the decision to take action and to make a positive change in their life. Clearly you are one of these people, and I want to congratulate you for reading this book.

As you know my name is Kenny Chapman, and I have made it my life's mission to empower people like you to turn their dreams into reality. But what you may not know about me is how I arrived at the place I am in today.

I have had the privilege of owning many different companies in several different industries in my lifetime. I have built a multi-million dollar market leading service business. I have become a top-rated international speaker and business development trainer, and I have had the opportunity to make a contribution to the success of thousands of people. And most of all, I have created truly meaningful relationships with the most important people in my life. I have even found exactly the kind of marriage I always dreamed of.

I don't say all this to brag or to make myself sound better than you or anyone else. As you will soon learn, the only difference between who I once was and who I am now is a few simple choices made over a period of time. These choices were based on strategies described in the book you now hold in your hands.

You see, I grew up with what I now call the "Us" and "Them" mentality, "Us" being the people that had to watch our money and work very hard for very little, and "Them" being the people who were educated, who drove luxury cars, and who lived in fancy houses. The "Thems" seemed to have all the things I wanted to have in my life, but didn't know how to get my hands on.

But what I did know was this: for my own sake, and the sake of my future family, I had to learn. I didn't know *how* I was going to do it, but that did not matter. What mattered was that I had the passion and the drive to keep pushing myself to learn what I had to learn, to do what I had to do, and to become the person I had to become. All that mattered was to never feel like one of "Us" again.

What I found was that there is a very simple and powerful method that works *every single time* I decide to create positive changes I truly desire in my life. This is the method I have made it my life's mission to share with people like you, my friend. It doesn't matter whether it is with your business, your relationships, your health, or your money, and it certainly doesn't matter what your current situation is.

If you have the desire and drive to create a better life for yourself, then you already have the power to create and accomplish anything you want. No matter where you are, or who you have been, there is no reason why you can't be more excited about your career, make more money, have more fun, enjoy better health, and build more fulfilling relationships. There is no reason why you can't jump out of bed every morning burning with the passion that will propel you toward your greatest dreams. This may sound cliché to you. I know it did to me before I began using the Six Dimensions to improve my life. Now I know that you can jump out of bed burning with passion every day for the rest of your life!

However, I am not here to tell you what you need to do with your life. Chances are, if you are reading this, you already know what you want. What I *am* here to do is to present you with a choice: a choice to implement a simple strategy I have used to empower myself and thousands of other people to make positive, lasting changes in their lives.

Let me ask you this:

What would your career, your family, your *life* be like if you could accomplish *anything* you ever set your mind to? As you are considering this, I want you to ask yourself how often you *really* think about where your life is going and why. How many more chances can you expect to get in your life, to read something that will help you incorporate principles to empower you, and to help you get everything you want?

Think about it, and you will realize that this is a rare moment in your life. Life is full of distractions, challenges, and all kinds of things that tear our focus away from our most important dreams. I want you to set aside any distractions you might be facing right now, and focus all of your attention and energy on *this* moment.

When you do this, you will begin to feel something come alive inside you. Something will begin to stir, to awaken, and to call out from the deepest place that is in you. That feeling, my friend, is hope. I want you to embrace this moment, to embrace that hope, and to give it the respect it deserves.

This is your life, and starting right now it is going to change forever.

So let's begin.

CHAPTER 1

The Six Dimensions of Change

L et me tell you why I know that the Six Dimensions of Change *can* and *will* alter your life. First of all, they are not things I learned from reading a book. They are not things you are going to learn from reading any book, even this one. What this book will do is *prove* to you once and for all that you already possess the Six Dimensions in yourself. It is going to help you uncover them and use them to your advantage, just as I have done in my own life.

As you already know, there are many books on the market that promise to have the solution for changing your life and turning your dreams into reality. Certainly, a lot of them are really great and can help you to make positive changes. However, there is one major difference between *this* book and the other personal development literature on the market.

The difference is that the Six Dimensions are not simply techniques you memorize and apply in order to achieve the results you desire. Rather, the Six Dimensions actually have the power to awaken the person you were born to be. They deal with the deeper issues of character that are essential to the achievement of long-term success and fulfillment.

When it comes to success, all you have to do is apply the formula to get what you want. Sure, some of it has to do with who you are. But with the right strategy, just about anyone can go after what they want, and get it. However, when it comes to sustaining and *enjoying* that success, it takes true character to get the job done. This is the foundation upon which the Six Dimensions of Change have been established.

The long-term success and fulfillment that come from living a life of passion and purpose have everything to do with who you are. The great motivational speaker and best-selling author Zig Ziglar once said that you can't outperform your self-image. Sure, you may be able to for a time, but in the long run your consistent actions and the inevitable results of those actions all stem from your self-image.

You see people all the time who have a tremendous amount of talent and who are blessed with great opportunities in life. Yet if they do not have the character to sustain success, they either fail to take advantage of it, or they don't keep it for long. Have you ever seen someone like this? Perhaps you have even been like this at times in your life. I know that I have.

Before I found some clarity about what was *really going on in my life,* I was at a point where I had achieved some outward success, but I can honestly say that I had not discovered what it means to be fulfilled and passionate about life. What I mean by "outward success" is this: I was in the top 5% of all income earners in the United States, I had freedom from my business, I had the custom home in the great neighborhood, I drove nice cars, and so on. Like most of us, I was always seeking that feeling I thought was going to come from achieving the next goal, or the next level of personal accomplishment.

However, I can remember that I did not even feel comfortable in my own skin. I was not able to embrace who I was. I was not even aware enough of myself to enjoy the success that I had in my life. In fact, I used drugs and alcohol to numb myself to my discomfort about who I really was. But one thing I have come to realize is that when we numb ourselves to the negative feelings in our lives, we shut off awareness of our own passion and enthusiasm.

And then what? Well, just as I once did, you may begin to search for exterior solutions for restoring your passion. Maybe you buy a new car and get excited about it. You wash it and wax it every week and you have it detailed. You parade it around the neighborhood and show it off to your friends. You freak out at your kids or your spouse when they spill something on the seat or when they shut the passenger door too hard.

But then something happens.

Several weeks or months go by and that feeling the car gave you starts to wear off. After a while you find that you are not washing the car as much. You begin to lose the passion and excitement you had about it in the beginning. And so, you must go out to search for the next sugar rush to restore your sense of meaning.

Why does this keep happening?

Because it's not about the car, it's about you, my friend. It's not about the next personal goal or the new career or the bigger paycheck or the new house. All of these things can be acquired, but if you don't make deep changes in your character, then you will never get a true sense of fulfillment from any of them. This change of character is what the Six Dimensions of Change will empower you to make.

True success is more the *result* of a healthy self-image than it is the *cause* of one. This is the point where you need to begin, regardless of what you own, or what you may or may not have accomplished in your life. Too often we postpone our own happiness until it can be validated by some kind of external circumstance. In reality, this validation can only come from within us.

But there is one thing I want you to keep in mind as we move through the Six Dimensions of Change: in spite of the fact that this book is about change, it is absolutely crucial that you embrace life as it comes, and live in the here and now. It is possible to pursue success with such intensity that you neglect to enjoy the experience of life itself.

The Six Dimensions of Change will empower you to discover who you truly are and to become a person who will create success as a natural result of living a life filled with passion and purpose.

Clarity – Habit – Action – Never Give Up – Gratitude – Enthusiasm

Clarity begins with knowing what you really want and who you must become in order to have it. Then you must form the Habits that will empower you to become the person you envision. The Actions you take will bring about the results you are after. Then you must learn to Never Give Up, no matter what, until you get what you are after. Finally, developing an attitude of Gratitude and Enthusiasm insures your enjoyment of all the good that comes into your life.

These are the Six Dimensions of Change I have discovered as a result of a determined, lifetime search. These are the Six Dimensions you are about to have awakened in you.

As we progress through them, remember that, unlike the application of techniques, the formation of character is a process. This is why it is so important to acknowledge and to live in the here and now. If you can do this, I promise you that you *can* and *will* accomplish anything you want in your life.

In fact, while we are talking about what you want, let's do a quick exercise. Stop reading right now and take about five minutes to write down the three primary things you want to accomplish in the next year. If you want, you can make one of them a personal goal, one of them a career goal, and one of them a goal that contributes something to other people. Don't hold yourself back, and don't wonder how you can accomplish these things right now. Just write them down without any attachment to how they will happen.

Keep your goals simple for now; we'll elaborate on this information later. Your goals might sound something like: lose ten pounds (personal), get a $5000 raise (career), and participate in three community fundraising walks (contribution). Simply word them in a way that makes sense to you.

This is going to provide you with the focus you need to take on the challenges in the next chapter. Go ahead and do it right now.

My 1-year Personal Goal: _Be able to bench 225 pounds._

My 1-year Career Goal: _Earn $20,000_

My 1-year Contribution Goal: _Give $200 Dollars to the church_

CHAPTER 2

Consciousness
Waking up to Your Dreams

Imagine this: you are on your way to work. You know if you are late again there is no way you will keep your job. You struggle to arrive on time, but there is just so much traffic. Suddenly, you realize there is an ocean you have to cross to get to work. You have no idea how you are going to do it, and you begin to panic. In desperation you try to drive your car through the ocean, but you realize there is no way you are going to make it. You get out and start to swim, but then you notice that there is a school of sharks circling the place where your office is. You swim faster, hoping you can slip past them unnoticed. But then you realize you are swimming through thick mud, and going slower and slower. You also realize you have floppy clown shoes on, and you are having trouble swimming because of them. Through the office window you can see your boss standing at your desk with a stop watch and a box to put your belongings in.

What are you going to do?

If you are stumped, let me make a suggestion: Wake Up!

Stop and think about this for a moment: the ocean was never there before. Never in your right mind would you try to drive your car through the ocean anyway. Not only that, you may have noticed that things just started getting weirder and weirder. Obviously you were not dealing with *real* circumstances.

However, how many times have you had dreams like this and not realized you were dreaming? All the time, of course.

And what do you do?

You continue to attempt to deal with the circumstances of your dream as if they were real. You struggle, become afraid, even panic, believing that you *must* do something to deal with circumstances that are not even real. If you were able to stop for a second and realize "Whoa! None of this makes any sense. I must be dreaming!" your actions would change *instantly!*

Even though this is true, the majority of us go through our lives largely unconscious, accepting the circumstances of our life as they come. Things happen that we don't want to happen, and they keep happening. Yet we keep dealing with them as they come, accepting the circumstances of our lives and dealing with crises that we accept as being unchangeable reality!

Most of us never stop for a second to question *what* we are doing, *why* we are doing it, or whether we are even dealing with the real issues of our lives! This is what I call being largely unconscious: living inside a dream that we could *wake up* from any time we wanted to. All we have to do is stop and say, "Wait. Is this really the way things have to be, or can I *do something* to change it?" We must be very careful to be completely honest here. Sometimes we attempt to justify things and tell ourselves stories about not being able to change something, when we actually can if we want to badly enough. Let's be *very* clear:

We *always* have a choice!

Have you ever had one of those moments when you were able to "wake up" when you were dreaming? Maybe one of those dreams where you are back in high school at age thirty-five because you still have a class to take before you can graduate? Sounds silly, right? You know that as *soon* as you realize it's not real, the nightmare is over and you are back in control.

Guess what? It's time to wake up and regain control of your life.

Let me ask you a few questions:

- Have you ever had that feeling around New Year's Eve that the year just raced by without you knowing where it really went?

Sure, all of us have. And most of the time, we can't think of even TEN THINGS that happened to us during that year! What about all the things you swore you were going to do, like get out of debt, find a new job, spend more time with your family, lose weight, start your new business. How many of those things happened?

This wondering at the end of the year is the result of living your life largely unconscious. At any time during the year you could easily have woken up and decided to start *making* things happen. However, you were too busy being distracted by the everyday cares of life.

- Have you ever gotten a bonus check or tax return and wondered where the money went after it was gone?

What happened to that money? Again, not knowing is a result of living your life largely unconscious.

Things happen *to* you: they keep happening and you keep wondering, *"What happened?"* Money, particularly, is something that can slip right through our hands without our having *any* idea of where it went.

- Have you ever stepped on the scale and freaked out because you gained thirty pounds?

When did it happen? I can tell you this much: I doubt it happened overnight, or even in a week. In fact, it happened over a long period of time, without you even being *aware* of it. Maybe you said, "Ah, I was good today with my diet, so I'll treat myself to a milkshake." No big deal, right? But over a period of time such exceptions become the norm. As Zig Ziglar said, "Exceptions are the most dangerous things we face in life, because they get us off track."

Most of the time, in the case of our health, we look for a quick way to get ourselves back into shape, which only does more damage to our body. Physical health plays a vital role in creating the life we desire. If our health is out of balance, it's very difficult (if not impossible) to maintain balance in the other key areas of our lives. I know from personal experience, because I spent most of my life battling my weight and health. My wife and I have created an extremely simple and effective weight loss and nutrition plan that we've used to maintain a healthy weight for years now. If you'd like to learn more visit www.the6stepdiet.com.

- Have you ever realized that your relationship with someone you love has fallen apart, and you don't know when or how it happened?

So many marriages end up this way, and when they do, no one seems to know precisely *when* it happened, or how it happened.

It is like the story about the frog in the pot of water: the heat was turned up gradually, and the poor thing remained in the water until he cooked to death. This is how we are with our relationships, and almost everything else in our lives, when we are largely unconscious. We are clueless, and powerless to guard ourselves against the termites that eat away at our respect, love and appreciation for each other. One day we may finally "wake up," only to find that it is too late to turn back.

Well, guess what?

That's not good enough anymore! You deserve better than to have your entire life pass you by, your money leave you, your relationships fail, your health deteriorate, and your dreams go to the grave with you.

It's time to wake up and take control, starting right now!

Hear this loud and clear, my friend:

Living your life largely unconscious is *never* going to help you reach your full potential and live the life you have always dreamed of. You have got to start paying attention to what you are really focusing on, and why. Your life is going to become the things you pay attention to, whether you want that or not.

Don't believe me? Think about this:

DON'T PICTURE A PINK ELEPHANT!

Now what are you thinking about? Right.

What you have to do is begin to build a vision in your mind and heart of what you want. Begin to build a clear and direct plan for how you are going to accomplish it. This is going to give you something to focus on other than what is happening to you right now. It is going to empower you to *wake up* and become aware of what you are doing. It is going to show you whether what you are doing now is going to help you get what you *really* want!

Here is the first thing you are going to do:

- Pay attention to how you feel

This is the only part of this book where I am going to encourage you to focus on the negative. Understand that there's really no good or bad, it's simply information for us to use. Many times we focus too much on whether or not something is "good" or "bad." Don't worry about failure or negativity, because it's simply feedback about actions that you're taking or that you have taken. You're either getting a result you want and feeling good, or you're not getting a result you want and feeling bad. If you're not getting the results you want, just acknowledge that the negative feeling is *there* in order to show you where you are off track. You see, there are times when positive thinking can be just as much an issue as negative thinking. If your life is not meeting your expectations right now, there is no point in saying, "Oh well, things really aren't that bad – it could be worse."

That is a dangerous way to think. You have to wake up and start listening to what those negative feelings are telling you. You have to confront the reality of where you are right now, so that you can *do something* about it.

Are you in pain? Find out why and do something to change it. Ask yourself what you need to do to feel *great* again. Or ask yourself what the source of your pain is and focus on doing the opposite. Think of your feelings as a guidance system to tell you what actions need to be taken to get what you really want.

• Pay attention to your habits

An experiment was done with a group of monkeys in a large habitation. In the middle of the habitation was a rope, which led up to a bunch of bananas that hung from the ceiling. However, every time the monkeys climbed the rope a fire hose would blast them off. After a while they stopped trying and just accepted the idea that the bananas were unreachable. At this point, the experimenters began to remove one monkey at a time and put a new monkey in to replace it. Of course, the new monkey would try to climb the rope, but the others would pull him right down to protect him from the hose. Eventually EVERY monkey was brand new to the habitation, and none of them had ever been blasted by the fire hose. But because the other monkeys pulled them down when they tried to climb the rope, they too accepted the idea that the bananas were unreachable.

Think about this as it relates to the habits in your life:

How many things are you doing now that are part of a learned pattern? Look at every single action and routine, every thought, and even the *beliefs* that have become habits in your life. Examine each one of them and ask yourself, "Is this going to help me to get what I *really* want?" Ask yourself where you acquired the belief or habit. Chances are that these things are not even relevant to your life. Ask yourself *who* you are modeling. Chances are that the person you learned these things from is not getting the kind of results you want for your life, either. If this is the case, then it is time to wake up and change things.

• Become aware of how much fear runs
  your life

Fear is not bad or good. It's simply your body's way of preparing you for something potentially damaging. It may be a situation that requires you to pay special attention to keep yourself from harm. However, there are times when we mistake excitement for fear. In other words, going on that roller coaster ride or first date, or starting that new business might be very exciting. It might even be something you *have* to do, but if you mistake the excitement for fear, it is likely that you are not going to do it at all. Either way, you need to find out how much fear is really running your life.

Let me give you an example: did you know that people are more afraid of public speaking than they are of death? Think about that for a moment: that means people are more afraid of failing and making fools of themselves in front of other people than they are of dying! I am not saying you should become a public speaker to overcome this fear. But what you do have to ask yourself is how much fear of the disapproval of others is really running your life. So what if you fail and you make a fool of yourself and your plans get foiled? You are still alive!

One of the businesses I own is a motivational speaking company. When I first began speaking in front of groups, I was absolutely terrified! What I discovered was that once I was on stage for a few minutes and realized nobody was going to throw things at me, I would settle down and relax a little bit. What was I afraid of? Not being liked? Not gaining approval? What other people would think? The truth is, it was a combination of all of these. Since I've confronted this fear, I do the very best that I can do, and give my audience everything I've got each time I take the stage. I am always able to positively impact my audience and receive consistently good reviews after a speech. Now I focus on the outcome I want, not what I'm afraid of. This makes all the difference in life.

Let me tell you the truth about fear. Once you confront it by doing what you are afraid of, then the fear evaporates like the stain of breath on a mirror. Fear is funny in that way. In fact, fear of the disapproval of others is an illusion brought on by the desire to appear perfect.

Deep in your heart, you know that perfection is impossible. Once you wake up and become conscious of this, everything changes. Once you wake up to what is *really happening* in your life and start asking yourself what you *really* want, you can begin to develop direction and purpose for your life. This direction will empower you to let go of uncertainty, to get focused and to become actively involved in your life!

Are you ready?

Great, because here is where we are going to start:

CHAPTER 3

Your Self-Image and You

Have you ever wondered if there was one single character trait that is common to all successful people? In case you have, I want to take this opportunity to introduce you to someone. But before I do, I want to ask you a question:

How much of your full potential do you believe is not being demonstrated in your life? You know, I have asked a lot of people this question. Some people say ten percent; some people say ninety percent. However, no one ever says zero. Maybe you can relate to this: pretty much every person you speak to wants to believe that the best part of them is still hiding up their sleeve.

Why is this? Well, without getting into the complications involved in such a question, let's look at the reality of this. How many beautiful people do you know who do not believe that they are beautiful at all? Do they act as though they are? How about people who have an AMAZING amount of intellectual capability and are doing nothing with it? Or what about people who have all kinds of amazing opportunities come into their lives but never take advantage of them?

Now let me ask you this: what good is all of this beauty and this talent and the opportunity if it is not taken advantage of? In a manner of speaking, they are not even real. I mean sure, they exist, but you can't do anything with them. It's like the person who buys a nice car but then obsesses over it so much that they never drive it for fear it will get damaged. What good is it? It's like that plastic fruit that looks so nice sitting on the table, but is of no use to you if you are hungry.

My friend, the point is that the good things we have in our lives are only good when they are helping to make our lives better and to make the world a more wonderful place. And guess what makes all of the difference?

Your self-image!

Remember, it is *impossible* for someone to outperform their self-image. You will only act as beautiful, talented, or intelligent as you truly believe you are. Sure, you may have times when you really shine in spite of your self-doubts. However, your self-image will always work as a correcting mechanism, readjusting to bring you back to a level of comfort consistent with your self-worth.

Think of it like cruise control on your car. You set it and there it stays at one constant speed. Sure, you can step on the gas for a while, but as soon as you take your foot off the accelerator you are going to end up right back where you were. You may know people who have a low sense of self-worth in regard to relationships. Do you know what happens when this kind of person finally finds someone who treats them right? That's right, they sabotage the relationship, or they do something to devalue the other person and convince themselves that the relationship is not worth keeping. The same is true in people's financial lives: Have you ever known a person who was always broke? What happens to that person when they get a raise, a promotion, or some kind of an inheritance check? They spend the money, and they are broke again.

When I was eleven years old, my father got a very large inheritance from my great aunt; I thought that was wonderful! He bought me a new motorcycle, we traveled to the Indianapolis 500, we ate out frequently, and so on. However, my father struggled with self-worth and it manifested through this inheritance (or money) just like it does with a lot of people. What I mean is, if your self-worth doesn't allow you to believe you're worthy of money, you will find a way to lose or spend your wealth. To make a long story short, my father was broke in only a few years, and spent the remainder of his life struggling for money. This was a great example for me. It reminds me of how I love my late father for showing me mistakes in life that I don't have to repeat.

As bizarre as these examples seem, there are countless others we could add to the list, and they are all demonstrations of the self-image at work. People adjust their consistent actions and their own level of success in their life according to what they believe they deserve. This stands at the foundation of self-worth. It's all about the amount of value we attach to ourselves. As long as you are living your life largely unconscious, your self-image is the cruise control, and you are asleep at the wheel. Let's change this now so that you can regain control of your life.

I want to introduce you to someone: the real you.

That's right. You see, here is the good news about your self-image: it is not who you really are. Rather, it is who you *believe* you are. Now this is not a book on philosophy. What I am talking about is the only part of you that is playing an ACTIVE role in your life. Any other kind of potential you may have means nothing unless you USE it.

What you are going to do is to wake up and take control of the wheel again. You are going to hit the accelerator and reset the cruise control. From now on, every time you strive for a new level and hit it, you are going to make sure that your self-image is set to keep you there. Until you make this conscious change, your self-image will keep holding you back. Personally, I spent many years thinking that I wanted to be a millionaire and have great relationships, but deep down I didn't believe I deserved it. Only once I got in touch with the "real Kenny" did things begin to take shape the way I wanted in my life. Now I live the life I deserve because I know I'm worthy of it. If you want to achieve more than you are achieving right now, it is going to require *becoming* who you were truly born to be. It all begins with your personal sense of value. Hear this loud and clear: the most common character trait of people who are successful is a healthy self-image.

The Six Dimensions of Change are going to help you to achieve this. However, we need to get a head start on it by discussing some of the unhealthy ways people determine their self-worth:

- Income

If you measure your self-worth according to your income, you can be sure that you will find yourself in a never-ending cycle: wanting more money but measuring your self-worth by the standard of what you earn, so that your sense of self-worth will never let you earn more than what you earn right now. Therefore, both your income and your self-worth will remain stuck in a "chicken or the egg" loop forever.

• Other people's opinions

This means for better or worse. Sure it is good to get validation from others, and we should never stop praising one another and believing the best about one another. However, giving someone the power to validate your self-worth is giving them way too much power and responsibility. No matter how much you love someone or how much they value you, people don't always act perfectly. There may come a time when someone is not so happy with you-that's absolutely ok and normal. These often are the times when your own wounded sense of self-worth can cause you to destroy the relationship out of hurt, guilt, or anger. Value and respect other people's opinions, but let your sense of self-value and self-respect belong to you alone. I used to struggle with this concept, wondering if I was being "selfish" or not. What I've come to learn is that this is being self-less, not self-ish. Honor and have compassion for other people and their opinions, but be who you are. You know who you are at the core.

• Appearance

This is quite possibly the greatest reason why people who are overweight can never get thin and stay thin. It is the same with your income. It can be another self-fulfilling prophecy loop that leads you to get out of debt only to gain it right back again. I was always the fat kid growing up. I would constantly struggle with my weight and I had created an identity around it. I used to say things like, "Well, this is my build; I'll never be skinny. I'm short and stocky like my father was built; it's just genetic." This is true. I am short and stocky like my father was, but it doesn't mean I have to be fat, carry a "beer gut," or lose my breath ascending a staircase. Now that I know who I am, I have found that if I continue to choose a healthy lifestyle and remain in balance, my body responds accordingly.

• Performance

This one is tricky. Sure, you want to accomplish great things with your life and you should never stop reaching for more. However, your accomplishments are going to be more the *result* of a healthy self-image than its *cause*. Let me repeat this because it is paramount. *Your accomplishments will always be more a result of a healthy self-image than its cause.* If you continue to attach your self-worth to what you have accomplished, failure is going to be crippling and the fear of failing will destroy your potential and your ability to take action.

You will also remain reliant on outside factors to validate your self-worth, rather than looking within yourself to discover the truth.

Failure is a key element in the process of success: you need to be able to maintain your sense of self-worth in spite of where you fail or even succeed. If you don't, your sense of self worth, your moods, your emotions, and your ability to live in the present and enjoy your life are going to be in a constant state of flux. Honestly, there's no such thing as failure anyway, there are only results. You either get a result you want (success), or you don't get a result you want (failure). We can label things however we want, but let's be honest about the fact that "failure" sometimes leads to our greatest awakenings and accomplishments in life.

Now, in case you are thinking that I have left you without a leg to stand on here, just hold on. It's time to step on the gas, my friend.

CHAPTER 4

Dimension #1: Clarity
The Roadmap to Making Your Dreams a Reality

Ben Stein said, "The first step to getting the things you want out of life is this: decide what you want." I mentioned before that most people live their life largely unconscious, and when it comes to that, lack of clarity is right at the core. A lot of personal development coaches will claim that most people do not know what they really want out of life. They will say that this is the reason so many people fail to get what they want. This is true. However, it is only a part of the story.

You see, everyone wants to be successful at *something*, even people who are afraid to do the work required to get them there. However, if you ask ten people what it really *means* to be successful you are probably going to get ten different answers. But at the very core of all of them, you'll find some kind of an emotional benefit: security, happiness, personal validation, or love. Most people truly *know* what they want out of life. The one thing that prevents their *getting* it is that they are not able to define it for what it is. Instead, they identify it as the feeling that comes when they buy a new car or get involved in a new romance or accomplish a personal goal. It's a feeling that is just as wonderful as it is unexplainable, and so they continue to chase the experiences that bring them that feeling.

As a result, most of us just bounce around as if we were in a pinball machine, chasing after the next thing we think will make us feel happier, more secure, or more alive. Little do we know that if we simply wake up and get some clarity about what REALLY brings those feelings to the surface, our whole life will change forever. This kind of clarity is what gives our lives a sense of meaning and direction.

This means it's more than clarifying *what* you want, it's about clarifying *where* you are now and *what* it is going to take to *get* you where you want to go.

Let me ask you this:

Have you ever been somewhere, gotten lost, and had to look at a map? Maybe it was some place like a park or a mall, where they have maps to help you find out how to reach your destination. What are the two things you have to know first? Well, surely you've seen those arrows that say "you are here." What if you didn't have that information to start with? Would it matter if you knew where you wanted to be, or even how good the map was? Of course not!

So as you see, in addition to having clarity as to what you really want, you have to be clear about where you stand right now. I am talking about being completely open and honest, perhaps painfully clear, about where you are. This isn't about judging yourself or your life. This is the necessary honest starting point in creating the real life you desire and deserve.

However, sometimes this is what really messes people up: when we *know* what we want and we even know *where* we are, but we are following the wrong map to *get* to our goal. In other words, we're clear about where we are and what we want, but, for whatever reason, we're following the wrong path because we're missing some vital information. For instance, someone who wants security may settle into a job simply because they think it is practical and stable. However, once they find that they really don't like what they are doing, they are going to start feeling restless. This sense of restlessness is going to rob the person of their security.

Or what if someone really WANTS to be in a great relationship or to get married, but they have no idea of what it really takes to establish and maintain that relationship? What if, instead, they follow the map that they saw their parents follow? What if their parents' *map* didn't work, but it is familiar, so they follow it by default? These are examples of knowing what you want, but failing to get it because of following the wrong map. This is normal, natural, and sometimes part of the learning and growth process. If you've followed the wrong map at some point (as I know I have), it's ok, be easy with yourself. Now you can do something about it!

So, what are we going to do?

Well, we are going to take each one of these: *where* you want to be, *where* you are now and your map for getting there, and we are going to get some real clarity. Most importantly, we are going to begin from this foundational point: your self-image.

Now here is how we are going to do this:

You need to clarify each of these details in such a way that you *truly* understand it. This means that you can explain it to *someone else* so that *they* can understand it. If you can *get* this kind of understanding about *where* you are, *where* you want to be and *what* it is going to take to get you there, then you are well on your way.

In short, if you can make something explainable it becomes more attainable.

Let's start with where you want to be. There will be four components to this:

- Self-Image
- Roles
- Actions
- Results

These are the four cores of clarity, and they are listed in the order of execution. As you now know, your self-image is the foundation. Next, you have the roles you play in your life, such as your role as a parent, a spouse or partner, a friend, an accountant, a boss, a coworker, or whatever it might be. At the core, each of these must be consistent with your self-image.

Why?

Because each of them requires certain habits and actions in order for the role to be maintained. As you know, these actions are driven by your self-image.

Next, we have the consistent *results* of those actions: more money, better relationships, a legacy as a philanthropist, a bigger house or a nicer car, happiness, security, a healthier body, you name it. This is where most of us start, and most of us get off on the wrong foot by working backwards to the actions, or even back to the roles. However, most of us never even consider the primary foundation of a healthy self-image.

We want better relationships and so we try to listen better and to spend more time with the people we care about. However, we don't focus on becoming the person we need to become in order to attract great relationships and to keep them. We want more money, but we don't focus on building the character that will empower us to *make* that money and, more importantly, to *keep* it and do good things with it, once we get it. On and on it goes. So here is what we are going to do, my friend:

Sit down right now and write down *the top 50 goals* that you currently have for your life. Let yourself go and don't edit, criticize, or even question *how* you are going to get these things. We'll get to that. This is an exercise in being honest with yourself about what you really want. Use these four areas to give you a starting point if necessary:

- Health
- Finances
- Career
- Relationships

If you can think of others, by all means have at it. The idea here is to be *honest,* so be sure that these goals are *yours* and that they are not driven by a need to prove something to someone else. For instance: if you really want a five-bedroom house on the harbor with a Jacuzzi and an indoor swimming pool, don't put down "build a shelter for the homeless" out of guilt. Make sure that you are honest with yourself. Besides that, if you make enough money to have your five-bedroom house, you'll probably be better positioned to help a charity, anyway. It may be difficult to come up with 50 goals right away, and that's ok. Challenge yourself, keep digging deeper, and let your imagination run until you have your list.

Once this is done, break your wants down into smaller pieces to create a timeline. Start with allocating a timeline for each of the goals. Choose 1, 5, or 10 years for now. Once you have this, refine your list so you have no more than 10 one-year goals. You can continue to build some timelines for your longer-term goals if you'd like, but we'll really focus on these 10 one-year goals for now. If you want to break down your longer-term goals, here's an example: if you aspire to founding your own private school for entrepreneurs in ten years, break it down to how far along you want to be in the next year, then the next five, and finally the next ten. As you are doing this, you can take your single most important goal in the areas of health, finances, career, and relationships, and break them down into smaller blocks.

Ok, ready for the next step?

Now we are going to go all the way back to your roles in relation to each one of these goals, and I want you to ask yourself this question:

What kind of person do I need to *be* in order to fulfill these roles and to have these things? This question is going to serve as the foundation for your new self-image. In reality, if you truly *want* something you have to define your self-image according to that something. Where you are now is just the residual of who you *were,* so let that go. *Your current situation is simply the result of choices and decisions you've made to this point in your life.* You already know the problem with using your current circumstances to define your self-worth. In reality there is only one healthy source for self-validation: your own freedom to choose, according to where you truly *want* to be.

Why?

Because your choice is the one thing that only *you* will ever control. The Jewish psychologist Victor Frankl, author of *Man's Search for Meaning*, called this "the last of human freedoms." Here is someone who survived the torment and humiliation of the World War II concentration camps. He realized that no matter what happened to him, his freedom of choice was the standard by which he measured his own worth. He knew that any day he could have been thrown into the incinerator with one hundred other people, or he could have been executed and his body would have been used to make soap.

Clearly, he was not valued as a human being. However, he did not see himself that way. Instead, he envisioned himself in a large lecture hall, instructing and inspiring others about the lessons in personal achievement that he learned as a result of surviving the torments of the camps. He began with the end in mind and decided to focus on using that standard to determine his value.

Now let me ask you this:

If he could do this in the midst of such circumstances, who will *your* vision of the future compel you to become?

Sit down and write a short paragraph to outline where you really want to be in the future. If you are at a loss, then find someone who has accomplished the same thing and study them. If it is someone you don't know, read about their life and find out what kind of a person they were. If you know them, start spending time around them or sit down and interview them. Do whatever you have to do in order to find out what kind of character traits got this person where they are.

This does NOT mean that you become a person you are not; the character traits I am referring to are most likely things that can be developed with practice. Were these people persistent, enthusiastic, decisive, kind, good listeners, empathetic, or resourceful? Whatever their traits, write them down. Then write down all of the things that made them that way. Together with the timeline, this is going to help you build a solid map to get you where you want to be in the future.

When I was just getting started in business as a young entrepreneur, I would call the most successful people in my town and offer to take them to lunch. Sometimes they would accept, and sometimes they wouldn't. I was persistent because I have always been driven by learning what traits and habits that successful people possess, and what they do differently than the masses do. Some of the tips I received from the people I spoke with became invaluable as I grew in life and business. Sure, some of them had traits I didn't care for, so I just took what I liked, and left behind what didn't fit for me and who I wanted to be. You can do the same thing.

Now, let's leave the map for a second and take care of the last step in getting clarity: where you are now.

Using the character traits from the last step, take an inventory of yourself and find where you are lacking. If you need to become a better listener, ask yourself how you are doing with this *right now*. If you really want to get clarity, take the time to ask a few people who really know you and who value you enough to be honest with you. Do this with *every* character trait and hold nothing back; there are no right or wrong answers, just truthful ones. Make sure you don't take anything personally, even if you hear things you don't want to. It's just information and it's all useful.

As you do this, you will begin to realize that what you have, what you do, and what you accomplish in life is not nearly as important as *who you become*. This is going to make all of the difference.

Are you beginning to realize that there are certain habits you will need to break in order to become the person you need to become? I know I did, and I still do. If you're realizing this, too, then we are right on track for the second Dimension of Change.

CHAPTER 5

Dimension #2: Habit
Your Internal Cruise Control

Let me start here by asking you another question: What percentage of a person's daily behavior is controlled by habit? Would you believe that it is as high as 85% in most cases? When you consider this, it's no wonder many of us are largely unconscious. In a sense we almost have to be, especially considering the amazing amount of information we are exposed to these days. We simply can't allow ourselves to be influenced by everything, or even to pay *attention* to everything we are exposed to. As a result, we shut down our awareness of the outer world and set the cruise control.

The problem is that occasionally we wake up, perhaps around April 14th or New Year's Eve, or the day of our wedding anniversary. In some cases we may even be faced with some kind of a crisis such as financial disaster, or the failure of a business or a relationship. It's only then that we look back and say, "How in the world did that happen?"

I'll tell you how it happened: YOU did it!

That's right, your consistent habits over a period of time brought about those results. First you develop your habits, and then those habits develop into behaviors and beliefs. Eventually they determine your lifestyle and experience. Taking a look at your life right now, ask yourself whether you are happy with the results. If you are happy, ask yourself if there is another level of fulfillment you want to reach.

Guess what?

The habits that got you where you are today are not going to get you where you want to get in the future. But here is the good news:

If you can begin to change your habits *today* according to where you really want to be in the future, you can create an entirely different experience for yourself. It starts with the person you have to become in order to get there. Now I am going to say this again because it is *so* important: it is ideal if your self-image is based on who you need to become in order to get what you want. Instead of thinking about what you think you can do, or what you deserve, start focusing on what you really want. Too many people never go after what they want because they don't believe that they deserve it. This held me back for many years of my life.

So what?

Since when does deserving have anything to do with it? People get things every day that they don't "deserve," for better or for worse. That's life. In reality, deserving really doesn't mean a whole lot, anyway. Yes, it's nice to get something good that you feel you deserve. And yes, it feels horrible when you get something bad that you don't believe you deserve. But in the end you are left with the option of dealing with such things as they come. There is no point in depriving yourself of something wonderful based on the assumption that you don't deserve it. In addition, no value exists in dwelling on the fact that "so and so" got something they didn't deserve, or they're so "lucky," and so on. Simply decide what it is you want, and let's get to work on developing the habits that you need to make you the person who can achieve it.

This is going to require a basic understanding of how to transform ineffective habits into effective ones. Notice that I did not call them "good" and "bad" habits. This is because you may already have some habits that are not "bad," but that are not going to empower you to get what you really want out of life. Instead, we are going to think of habits in terms of effective or ineffective. For instance, it may not be "bad" to sit in front of the TV for three hours every night. However, is this habit going to be effective in helping you to become the person you need to become? Once I had accomplished a certain level of freedom in finance and business, I found myself golfing almost every day, and "distracting" myself in other areas that limited my personal growth and ability to achieve a new level of goals. There's nothing wrong with golf or other fun activities. Just check in with yourself to make sure you're not using anything to distract yourself, as I did with playing golf.

Sit down right now and go through your entire routine for the day, the week, or even the month if you have to. You may even want to keep a journal on yourself for a while. As you do this, examine every habit in your life as it relates to the goals you came up with in the last chapter. Then ask yourself this question:

"Is this habit going to help me become the person I need to be, in order to fulfill the role, take the actions, and get the results I am after?"

If not, make a decision TODAY to change things. Don't dwell on or worry about the past, and don't "kick your own butt" over previous actions or behaviors. Don't worry about how you are going to do it yet. We will get to that.

You may also find yourself wanting to rationalize or minimize the severity of the habit. Don't use "softeners" to minimize behaviors, and certainly don't compare yourself to the masses. If your friends go drink beer every night, it may seem ok if you do it too. Ask yourself if these people have accomplished the same things you want in your life. This is a good way to put your habits in check. No matter how small the habit may seem, remember: termites do more damage than hurricanes, fires, and earthquakes combined. Never underestimate the power of a small, repeated habit or routine over a period of time. If it is not going to help you reach your goal, make a decision to stop the madness.

This is your life, and today is the only day that you will ever be able to make a change. If you find that you fall back into a habit that you've been trying to change, simply catch yourself, acknowledge it, and start again. Don't worry about changing this habit for the rest of your life; just shoot for 30 days in a row. If you slip, then simply start again and begin a new 30-day habit.

The purpose of this step is to move you past the first stage of what I call "habit transformation." The process looks something like this:

- Unconsciously ineffective
- Consciously ineffective
- Consciously effective
- Unconsciously effective

In the "unconsciously ineffective" stage, you are largely unconscious, basically going through life with the cruise control on, and totally unaware of where your habits are taking you. Again, to some degree this is a defense mechanism against the onslaught of information we are exposed to in our everyday lives. However, if your habits are not helping you become the person you need to be in order to get what you really want, then you need to become aware of them in order to change them.

This is the stage of becoming "consciously ineffective," where you recognize the habits that are ineffective in getting what you really want out of your future. This is truly a great step because you are learning and becoming aware of what's not working for you. We must realize these things in order to take control of our actions.

Now, are you ready for the hardest part?

This is the "consciously effective" stage, and this is where most people want to give up.

Why?

Well, because it is during this stage that you are going to find yourself slipping between the "consciously effective" and "consciously ineffective" stages of the habit transformation process. This is perfectly normal; you have to give yourself the room and the permission to fail and to mess up sometimes. Think about it this way:

Have you ever seen a baby learning to walk? They struggle to get up, leaning on something the entire time. Finally, they find their balance and take the first step. And then what happens? Well, they fall and they get hurt and they cry. But then what?

They get back up and they try again, and again and again. They can fall a dozen or more times in one day, but they still get back up and try again. Think about that: we are talking about a baby.

Yet what do we *adults* do when we fail at something? We get angry and frustrated and upset, we call ourselves all kinds of names and we kick ourselves while we are down. Talk about role reversal!

So as you enter into the next stage of habit transformation, just accept in advance that you are going to make mistakes…a lot of them. That's ok. The bigger mistake is keeping the cruise control on until you drive right off the edge of a cliff. I've often said I've made more mistakes than most people in life…because I've taken a lot of actions in many different areas. They're not mistakes as long as you're taking action and learning from the outcome.

Your next step is going to be to take all of the character traits you came up with in the last chapter, all of the habits you found in the person you are modeling yourself after, and in a way step into that person's skin. In Hollywood, they call this method acting: the practice of actually *pretending* that you are the character you are becoming in the film.

Does it work?

Well, an example of a modern-day method actor is Brad Pitt. They say that during the filming of *Interview with a Vampire* he became so wrapped up in the darkness and despair of his character that he sank into a deep depression that lasted the better part of a year. This is a prime example of how someone can move from the conscious stage of habit transformation and become deeply entrenched in the unconscious stage. In this case, I would regard the habits as very effective in getting Brad into his character, but grossly ineffective in helping him to maintain a healthy lifestyle.

This is an example of how ineffective habits get formed. You see, there was a brief time in his life when the dark and depressing characteristics were effective in helping him to get into character. However, habits can be hard to break and we often hold onto them *long* after they have become ineffective.

That said, you are going to need a way to remind yourself to be aware of when you are moving from your new effective habits back to your old and ineffective ones. One example is the story of a man who actually carried an index card in his back pocket to keep track of every time he slipped back into his ineffective habits.

This was a guy who found that he was making self-deprecating remarks whenever he was around an attractive woman. He would even say things to take a stab at her, and end up turning her off completely. His goal was to get into a great relationship, and he realized the negative remarks were being made out of a fear of being rejected. He was rejecting himself, and her, before she got a chance to do it. Talk about an ineffective habit.

He came to realize that if he could stop himself long enough to take an index card out of his back pocket and make a mark on it, then he could stop and change his behavior. In seven days, he broke a lifelong habit and has never gone back. Now, there are times when it may take longer than seven days. That's ok. The point is to find something that will help you to interrupt the negative pattern so that you can remind yourself to get back on track.

You can get really crazy with this one. I have seen people who would literally say the word "cancel" or "reset" out loud. Of course, other people would wonder what they were up to and they would have to tell them. This is good. The more people around you who are aware of your determination to break your ineffective habits, the more difficult it will be for you to turn back. If you find yourself becoming depressed, you can get up and run around the block, or do twenty jumping jacks or some pushups. You can do a silly dance or, if you are in public, you can look around at everyone and picture them as cartoons.

Whatever it is, make sure that it is something that stops your old habit dead in its tracks. Once this is done, you in effect fire a missile at that old habit by immediately replacing it with a new one. The best way to do this is to choose a habit that sends you in the exact opposite direction. For instance, my buddy with the index card would turn around and pay the attractive woman some kind of compliment. If you find that your habit is watching TV for three hours a night, get in your car, drive to the park, and go for a walk. Or go out and work in the yard for the next hour, or take your spouse out on a date.

Whatever it is, commit to interrupting the ineffective habit and correcting course immediately by engaging in the effective one. Sound easier said than done?

Well, that's why we need to move on to the third Dimension.

CHAPTER 6

Dimension #3: Action
Step on the Gas and Drive

L et me ask you a question: how likely are you to get in front of a moving truck to try to stop it? You'd have to be LARGELY unconscious for that one, my friend. However, what if the truck was still in park and the driver was about to put their foot on the gas? The point here is that it is a lot easier to stop someone who has not started moving yet than it is to stop them once they have some momentum going. So, what is the key to momentum?

Action!

A great deal of success literature deals with the power of positive thinking and the changing of your beliefs in order to better align yourself with what you want. However, nothing in this world happens without action. Let me say that again: *Nothing in this world happens without action.* It is action that brings about results, and all the positive thinking in the world is not going to change that. In fact, sometimes the more you sit and think about something the harder it gets for you to take action. You start thinking about all of the things that can go wrong, you start to worry, that worry turns into fear, and pretty soon you are not doing anything at all.

Let me save you the trouble when it comes to fear and worry: if you take action, things are going to go wrong sometimes. At first, they may go wrong a lot of the time. But this is no reason to stand by and do nothing. In fact it is the best reason to take action.

Why?

Because you are going to learn a lot more by *doing* than you could ever dream of by *thinking* about something. Let me ask you this:

Have you ever studied something in a classroom, trained to do a job, or practiced a sport for months in preparation for a game? What happened when you started the job, or when game day came and that first whistle blew?

You forgot everything you knew, didn't you? You know how it is, you get that "deer in the headlights" thing going on, and you ask yourself: "What *have* I learned in the past few months?"

The truth is that you *learned* a lot. But there is a difference between learning and applying what was learned.

When you play those first few games, or face those first few weeks on the job, you often find that it is like starting the learning process all over again.

You may make all kinds of mistakes, but you learn how to correct them very quickly. And you learn how to avoid making them again. Not only that, everything you learn from your failures and your successes has some kind of emotional context attached to it. This increases the impact of the learning experience. You learn with a conviction that is just not part of the classroom experience. This is where the pursuit of perfection can become a dream killer. You build a picture in your mind of the perfect future, the perfect relationship, or the perfect career. And that's great.

However, when it comes to actually *making it happen* in real life, your dream comes under the harsh scrutiny of reality. And the only way it is going to survive is if you can allow it to get a few dings and dents along the way.

For instance, you may have the dream of becoming a freelance writer. You may be thrilled at the idea of not having to deal with the hassle of ringing alarm clocks, long drives, or screaming bosses. And as long as you are not doing anything to make the dream *really* happen, you don't have to discover all the little pimples that will surface during its adolescent stage.

But once you start taking action, things *are* going to go wrong, and you may find out that there is more work involved than you imagined. There may be challenges you are not prepared for. Your dream may get dragged through the mud a few times before it gets its chance to shine.

That's ok. Better to risk that than to sit and do nothing for fear your dream will lose some of its appeal. The point is: in order to move from the "thinking about it" stage to the "just do it" stage, you are going to have to risk a few bumps in the road. It's actually a blessing in disguise that we don't know the real difficulty or all the challenges we may face with a new venture, or we would probably never take any action at all. The good news is that as you learn, take action, and start building momentum, the law of probability is going to come to your rescue.

The law of probability basically states: the more out, the more in.

This means you will make more mistakes by doing something than by doing nothing; however, you will also achieve more results.

In sales this is called the "law of averages." It means the more people you contact, the more presentations or pitches you will be able to make. Usually you will have this opportunity with ten out of every one hundred people. The rest are going to ignore you, or cut you off once they realize you are selling something.

Out of those ten presentations, at least one person is going to buy from you. Now, this does NOT mean that if you are a lousy salesperson, lacking people skills and product knowledge, you are guaranteed to make a sale. However, I bet if you take strenuous action and contact as many people as you can, you are going to learn *really* fast exactly what you are doing wrong. Then it is only a matter of time before you get the hang of it. This is the key to success… massive action!

Your other option is sitting in a classroom, learning, studying, and memorizing. And all that is great. But without action, you have no way to develop the talent to apply what you have learned. Living in Colorado, outdoor sports are a big part of life. I can read a book about skiing or fly-fishing, but until I get on the slopes or out on the river and actually do the activity myself, I'll never have the real experience. All areas of our lives are exactly the same: they take practice and effort.

You see, it is typical for us to look at a successful person and think they are so good at what they do that they never fail. However, when you study the lives of successful people, you begin to realize that they all have something in common: all of them had massive amounts of "failure" under their belts as a result of taking action to achieve their goals.

A good example is the great baseball player Ty Cobb, who was well known for his ability to steal bases. What you almost *never* hear about is how many times he *failed* trying to steal a base. He had more failures under his belt than anyone else in the game.

But is that what people remember him for?

Of course not. They remember his success.

Another example is Thomas Edison, with his famous ten thousand failed attempts at creating the light bulb. He probably had more consecutive failures than anyone else who attempted the same kind of thing. Yet once he hit the nail on the head, none of those failures meant anything.

The Nobel Prize winning physicist Niels Bohr said that an expert was a person who had made all the mistakes that could be made in a very narrow field.

This may not be very encouraging, but when you think about what he is really saying it gives you a better understanding of the role failure plays in becoming a success. You see, as much as we are afraid of failure, what we have to realize is that we actually take risks all of the time.

Let me give you an example:

Around the same time I was writing this book, the pilot of a commercial airliner had a heart attack and died while the plane was still in the air. Thank God for copilots. But think about this: you are taking a risk when you get on a plane.

You are counting on the fact that your pilot is going to remain alive. You risk your life whenever you get into your car and drive, or when you go for a swim at the beach. You take risks all the time, but the potential danger is far enough from your mind that you are more focused on the present moment than on something that *might* happen.

The point is this, my friend: if you want to succeed at anything, you are going to have to risk failure. In fact, you are going to have to give yourself permission to fail, and to forgive yourself when you do fail. You are going to have to persist, and move past your failures. The world has a way of forgiving people who take initiative sooner than they will tolerate someone who is all talk and no action. Remember, there's no such thing as failure anyway – only results. People, and life in general, also have a peculiar way of making room for someone who is willing to take risks in order to get what they want. If you can demonstrate that you know where you are going and are determined to get there no matter what, you become like a truck barreling down the highway at full speed. It is less likely that someone is going to get in your way or try to stop you if they see that you are already in motion. The fact of the matter is that most people are looking for a truck being driven by a successful, positive, action-oriented person, so that they can jump in and enjoy the ride of life.

The same is true with fear: it is more likely to overcome you when you are at rest than when you are in motion. What I am talking about now, my friend, is momentum. When you are moving toward your goal, you are a cause set in motion.

Sure, you may stumble. You may hit a few obstacles, or have to correct course and change your direction at times. However, if you have a substantial amount of momentum going, you are not going to have anywhere near as much trouble staying in motion.

Let me ask you a question: how many times have you tried to steer a car while it is sitting still? Not so easy to do, is it? However, once you start moving and you have some momentum going, it is a lot easier to change direction. The same is true in relation to action and momentum: the more you have, the easier it is going to be for you to use it to change direction.

Why?

Well, first of all because it is going to be much easier for you to see where you went wrong. After all, if you are the one making the moves and making things happen, it means that you are the one responsible for repairing the damage and correcting course when something goes awry. As long as you are not taking *any* action, it is easy to sit by and blame other people – or even circumstances – for the lack of results in your life. Action raises the awareness of your responsibility, and puts you in complete control of your life and destiny.

But that's not all: it will also make it harder for you to stop or to give up. The harder you are working at something, the more you have invested in it. This means if you make a mistake you are less likely to call it quits. A good example of this can be found in my business coaching and consulting services. Often, the amount I'm paid is unimportant because I love to help people accomplish more than they ever thought possible. However, if there's a healthy fee for the service, rather than the service coming cheap or even free, then the business owner is much more vested in taking the recommended actions to get the desired result. Action immerses you in your plans, and brings what is inside you to the surface. Anyone knows the more actively involved you are in something, the harder it is to give up. Instead, you will focus your energy on correcting course and sending your momentum in the right direction.

Another thing that consistent action will do is to help you keep your eyes on the horizon, instead of being distracted by the obstacles that may get in your way. Picture this: it's night time, you get into your car, and you turn the headlights on, but all you can really see is the road in front of you. Since you don't know what is ahead, you just sit there. Sounds silly, doesn't it?

Well, I'll tell you this: allowing the current circumstances to keep you from moving toward your future is just as silly. Once you put your foot on the gas and start moving ahead you will see more of the road in front of you. And as long as you keep moving, your vision will stay one step ahead. This is the benefit of consistent action: it builds courage by helping you to keep yourself focused on what you really *want* out of your future, instead of being paralyzed by your present distractions.

Finally, the more momentum you have built up, the less effort you are going to have to exert to move forward. Have you ever seen a space shuttle take off? Did you know that there is more energy exerted in the first few minutes after liftoff than during the entire trip out into space and back?

This is because getting something started is always the hardest part. However, once you break friction and get moving, your momentum carries you to the next thing and the next thing and the next. This is the obvious key to keeping momentum: as soon as you finish one thing, move right on to the next, and just keep on going. The other option is to become complacent and stop once you have accomplished one thing. This can lead to "layover mentality," where you begin to justify inaction by waiting for circumstances to be perfect before you take the next action. Again, there's nothing wrong with taking a break, or waiting for a necessary step to be in place prior to your next action. Just make sure you're very clear with your plan and actions.

Anyone who has ever been stuck in a traffic jam knows how exhausting and frustrating that stop-go-stop-go mentality can be. Consistent action is the key to momentum and to getting positive results, over and over and over until you become unstoppable.

So how about it?

Are you ready to get this thing moving?

Great. Here is what we are going to do:

First, we are going to develop the right mindset for taking consistent action, using the following mental cues:

- Stop lying to yourself

If you are not taking action to move toward your goals right now, then you are not being honest with yourself about what you really want. Sure, you may be *telling* yourself that you want something with your words and your thoughts. However, being honest also requires being honest with your actions. What you have to understand is that inaction *is* action. It is the action of accepting failure in your life by doing nothing. It's the process of settling for less than you truly desire or deserve. This may not sound very positive, but I guarantee you that if you stop rationalizing and admit what is really going on, you will get yourself in gear more quickly. Be honest with yourself; don't "judge" or beat yourself up.

- Hold yourself accountable for results, not just for action

Ok, I realize that I have spent this entire chapter talking about taking action and now I am telling you to hold yourself responsible for results instead of *just* action. What I am giving you here is a warning against becoming busy but unproductive. I use this theme consistently to train the leadership team in my plumbing, heating, and air conditioning business. You can be very "busy" but very unproductive at the same time. Life and goals are not about how busy you are, but completely about how productive you are. As you begin to take the actions necessary to make your goals a reality, give yourself a pat on the back for getting started. However, you must begin right away to measure your actions against the results you want, to see if you are really getting where you want to go. If you are not, correct course *immediately,* or you may find yourself taking consistent actions that are not in alignment with your goals.

The objective here is positive and productive momentum: if you do not hold yourself accountable for the results of your actions, you may find yourself riding the spiral downward instead of upward. Your level of internal accountability is your compass. This is how you know your direction and find your real strength.

- Give yourself permission to stumble

Yes, I just told you to be accountable for results. This means your failures as well as your successes. You have to be careful to hold yourself accountable for failure in an intelligent way. This means that you view failure as an indication that your plans or actions need some correction. Most of the time, we hold ourselves accountable for failure by beating ourselves up and connecting our sense of self-worth to the failure. I spent many sleepless nights in pain, tearing myself down, based on what I viewed as failure in my life.

What does that accomplish? Clearly nothing productive or positive. It continues to undermine self-worth and is based on a false perception!

Instead, how about looking at failure as a positive signal that you need to correct course? Let's face it: you are *going* to fail sometimes, so you may as well give yourself permission. Otherwise you are going to stay stuck for fear of failing. Henry Ford had a great perspective when he said, "Failure is simply the opportunity to begin again, this time more intelligently."

Now, it's time to put together your plan of attack. What we are going to do is take the goals you have come up with and build an action plan.

In order to lay out your plan for action we are going to follow a simple acronym with the word PLANS:

Portions – Landmarks – Action – Negotiation – Synergy

Let's start with the first step.

• Portions

This means that you break your plan up into small portions so that you can work on each of them one at a time. You might have heard this referred to as "eating the elephant one bite at a time." It's great to have big plans for the future, but if you bite off more than you can chew you're going to choke before you even get to the main course.

Now, take each of your ten-year goals and let's begin to break them down into bite-size pieces. I believe in ten-year high-level goals or vision, but it can be tough to break these lofty goals into actions that you can take today to move toward those goals. I like to work with one-year and three to five-year goals, as they're a little easier to create an action plan around that can be implemented immediately. Regardless of which time frame you choose to work with, you must break them down month by month, week by week, and, finally, day by day. No matter what your goal may be, make sure that you are setting each goal with a long-term mission in mind.

Too often we set goals, achieve them, and then move on to the next one with no sense of a greater purpose. The more long-term your goals are, the more purposeful your short-term portions of the goals will become. While you are doing this, you will also want to incorporate the habits that you are working on changing as a part of achieving your goals.

• Landmarks

This means that you set landmarks along the way, as you move toward your long-term goal.

The purpose?

Celebration of your success.

You see, a lot of the time you will set a long-term goal and not give yourself permission to celebrate your successes along the way. This is a mistake, because you are robbing yourself of the incredible momentum that comes from celebrating your victories. Setting landmarks will give you something to look forward to, and will also create a sense of urgency that will compel you to action. Having specific landmarks will give you a reason to write your plans down and track your progress. It never ceases to amaze me how many people skip the step of writing down their plans because they don't think it is important.

On the contrary, writing your plans down is the very thing that *makes* them plans, and gives you something solid to set your sights on. This helps give you the emotional drive to pursue these desires. Never forget that the true reward is derived from the process, as life is simply a wonderful journey that connects our goals and actions along the way.

• Action

This is the part where you take action. This means that you get started right away, whether you are ready or not, and whether your plans are even *complete* or not. Too often we think that we have to have a complete plan before we start moving forward. This is a surefire way to invite procrastination into your life. In reality, the act of building your plan is *always* going to require a degree of trial and error, so get started right away. In the consulting work I've done, I've seen a lot of well-written business plans, but without action, they're simply good ideas on paper. Action is always the key to accomplishing what you want.

• Negotiation

This is where you examine your plans in light of your failures and successes, and continue to negotiate your approach. As you do this, you will want to make sure that you stay focused on the primary objective that is your long-term goal. Too often, we get this backwards. We rigidly stick with our plans and routines, even when they are not working. As a result, we arrive at our first landmark only to find that a slight miscalculation got us off track. Better to keep your *plans* flexible and continue to negotiate them according to whether they are moving you toward your specific goal. Again, this is the reason you have to take action right away and make negotiation a fundamental part of developing your plan.

• Synergy

This is probably one of the most important things you will ever do in pursuing your dreams: get some outside accountability. I don't care how self-sufficient and independent you are, you will *always* be able to accomplish more if you make yourself accountable to another person. The trick is going to be choosing the *right* person to be accountable to. Make sure that it is someone who is not too emotionally vested in the outcome, or even in your life. A spouse can be great as far as encouraging you, but they are not always likely to get in your face when the situation calls for it. Not only that, if they do, you may find your defenses going up when the most important person in your life decides to become your coach. It is better to find someone who has enough of an outside perspective to be brutally honest with you, but who at the same time cares enough to hold you accountable to follow through. If you are working on a goal along with your spouse, then find someone who can hold you *both* accountable.

When you do this, you also want to make sure the person is someone you respect, so that you will feel compelled not to let them down. The other thing this person can do for you is to provide you with a sounding board to evaluate your plans and determine where you need to correct course. Much of my success in life and business is attributed to the peers I've surrounded myself with who always tell me the tough truth about what they see happening in my life. You can also create a "personal board of directors," or join a mastermind group, if a group setting benefits you more than a one-on-one relationship.

So now what?

On to the next chapter?

I don't think so, not yet. Sit down RIGHT NOW and create a list of a few people you are going to be accountable to. It is *very* important to make sure you contact these people and get their permission. Make sure that they are prepared for the responsibility of being your accountability partners. If you get someone who does not really want the long-term responsibility, someone who says yes out of guilt or obligation, you may end up with a strain in the relationship.

Get this done now, and I'll see you on the next page.

CHAPTER 7

Dimension #4:
Never Give Up

The One Thing That Changes Everything

If there is any secret formula for being successful, I would have to say it could be summed up in these three words:

Never Give Up.

Never.

Got it?

Winston Churchill once delivered the following speech:

> "Never Give Up.
> Never Give Up.
> Never Give Up."

That was it.

Then he walked off the podium without a thank you or anything else.

Why?

Because he had come to learn, just as many others have, that this is the most crucial element of success. Yes, I told you that your self-image was the key and the foundation of success. But this is the reason: as long as you attach your self-worth to your failure, you are going to continue to lose momentum when you fail. However, there is something else you must continue to remember about "failure": it's just as much a part of the process of success as anything else.

That's right.

Most of us struggle with the idea of failure and create all kinds of positive affirmations in order to separate our sense of self-worth from our failures. We struggle to find ways to cope with failure and to move on from it. All of these problems can be solved by changing the way you think about failure.

Napoleon Hill said: "Failure cannot cope with persistence."

Why not?

Because there is no way to stop someone who has undying determination to succeed and who refuses to quit no matter how many times they may meet with failure. The great basketball player Michael Jordan said, "I never lost a game. I just ran out of time."

In case you never had the privilege of seeing this guy play, he would give it everything that he had right down to the last second. It did not matter how far behind his team was, he ALWAYS played to win. Not only that, even when he lost he never accepted it as defeat; he just acknowledged that he had run out of options to win by running out of time.

Now, take this into consideration and look at your life for a moment. Is there any failure that was so severe that you lost *every* option you may have had to succeed? Barring death or a life prison sentence, there is really nothing that can prevent you from persevering until you get what you want. Sure, there are obstacles, and setbacks, and all kinds of unexpected things can happen.

However, the people who never give up are the people who are consistently focused on what they want and who will stop at nothing to have it. Now here is the problem: it is easy to *tell* someone these things, but how do you really make them happen?

Well, let's go back to your habits for a moment. Are there any habits you have now that you had a hard time developing? We already mentioned one:

walking. But what about driving your car, reading, or doing what you do for a living? What about shaving, brushing your teeth, taking a shower, or eating a meal? As easy as all of these things may seem, there was a time when you were really lousy at them. How did you learn them?

By refusing to give up and by refusing to accept failure.

Think about it: when you were learning to drive, did you say to yourself: "I guess I'll give this a shot, but if it doesn't work out I can always walk everywhere for the rest of my life?"

Or how about when you were learning to eat your food? Yes, it may sound silly, but there was a time when you couldn't do it. Did you say: "Geez, I'll never get this right. I guess I'll just drink from a bottle until I die?" Of course not!

And what about learning to communicate with other people using words? What about learning to read or to write? You see, just about all of these things have one thing in common: we consider them to be non-negotiable. In other words, surrendering and accepting failure was just *not an option*. We didn't even stop to *consider* whether it was an option.

Why not?

Because we considered those things absolutely essential to our survival and we worked at them with diehard perseverance and determination. The fear of failure didn't even enter our minds, because we *knew* that all we had to do was get back up and keep working at those things until we finally got them.

And then what?

Well, we mastered those things and we became comfortable. Then, when we thought of a goal we really wanted to accomplish, we became paralyzed by fear and doubt. What's up with that?

But that's not all. We started to tell ourselves things like, "I'm just not disciplined enough," or "I'm just too lazy," or "I could never do___."

Says who? What would have happened if you had taken on that attitude in regard to learning to walk, talk, eat, drive your car, or do your job? Sounds absurd, right?

You see, my friend, the point here is that you have all the discipline and the drive you need to stick with something until you succeed. You've already proven it. The problem is the story that you keep telling yourself. What if instead you were to begin to treat your goal to lose weight or to build a better relationship with your spouse in the same way? What if you just *decided* that you were *going* to succeed no matter what you had to do and no matter how long it took? What if it was more an act of survival than something that "could be nice?"

I can tell you one thing that you would do:

You would start viewing failure as a means to learning what is *not* working, instead of viewing it as a horrible, confidence-crushing event that should be avoided at all costs.

In reality the only kind of failure is the decision to give up. This is the only way you can truly fail. Never give up!

So now that we have you in the right mindset, we need to develop a plan for making it a habit to never give up. Let's begin with the most important thing:

• Get Real

Make sure that the goal you are pursuing is consistent with who you truly are inside. Now, this is not some deep philosophical statement. What I am talking about is passion and enthusiasm. Are you in a job or a career that you chose simply because you thought it was the most secure, practical, or lucrative option out there? Did you choose it because you were "supposed to?" Are you doing it because someone else thought you *should*? Are you doing it simply because you did not *know* what you really wanted to do?

Look at every goal in your life and ask yourself honestly if it is something that is consistent with your source of internal drive. If not, you are going to find yourself struggling with mediocrity or even giving up at the first signs of defeat. You may be short-changing yourself by pursuing something that you don't really want because it is not connecting you to your true passion. And do you know what?

You are also shortchanging the people in your life. You have to understand that in spite of all the things you give people, the most valuable thing you can give them is the real you. If they do not want that, then they don't really care about you or who you are. The people who *really* love you would love nothing more than to see you truly come alive. Not only that, it would inspire them to follow your example, and other people would be inspired to follow *their* example. As Gandhi once said, "We must become the change we want to see in the world."

What I am saying is that you have a choice: you can either force yourself to keep going in the face of defeat by sheer willpower, or you can do something that is going to bring out your natural drive. As a person who made this decision a long time ago and has seen many others do the same, I can assure you about which choice will inspire you to never give up.

• Get Rid of Your Conflicting Agendas

This means you need to give yourself no option of surrender. I can't tell you how many people I have seen who choose to develop a backup plan and end up making that their primary plan. If you chase after two rabbits, you'll lose both of them. Most of us know this, but we deny it when we first start to build our dreams. We develop a backup plan we think will be "more practical," and then we end up letting our dream collect dust.

What does it mean to have no options of surrender?

It means that whatever you have going "on the side just in case," you need to let go of immediately. Think about it: what if *all* that additional attention and effort was directed toward your primary goal? This doesn't mean that directions won't or may not change many times in life; it's more about making sure that you're not using softeners and building a backup plan instead of going after what you truly want with all that you have.

Anthony Robbins really summed this up when he said:

"Stay committed to your goal, but stay flexible in your approach."

Let the flexibility be your backup plan, but never make a backup plan to replace your goal. In other words, take detours if you must, but no escape routes.

How much better would your chances be at success? In relation to a career, a lot of people make this mistake. Here is what you have to ask yourself: if you are dividing your attention between your goal and a potential escape route, how can you expect to compete with the person who has committed themselves one hundred percent? Better to become one of these people right now, so that you can commit everything you have to what you do.

• Protect Your Dream

There are always going to be people in your life who doubt you, or even try to discourage you. Sometimes these are the people whose support you need the most. They may discourage you from pursuing your dreams in the name of family duty. However, as Napoleon Hill said: "Duty does not subject you to the destruction of your personal ambitions." Remember, the people in your life are going to benefit the most from you being the best person you can be.

All of the money and security in the world is not going to change that.

What you have to understand is that the influence of other people can either make or break your success. Your job is to protect yourself and your dream from negative influences. If you know people who never have anything positive to say about taking risks or pursuing ambitions, don't tell them about your goals. If you find that turning on the news and hearing about the hard economic times, or anything else, is discouraging you from taking action to build a better financial future or start a new business, turn it off. What you have to do is to make your life an incubator for your dreams: a place where they can grow and thrive. You need to build up power, momentum, and enthusiasm, without having to fight off negative influences.

This might mean you have to draw some boundaries with certain people. You may even have to ignore some of them. However, as you practice the principles in this book and really start to get results, you'll find that the people who *really* care about you will come around. Several years ago, I made a personal choice to leave a long-term relationship and pursue what I truly wanted and desired in a relationship. This choice made many of my closest friends and relatives highly uncomfortable. Some of them thought I'd lost my mind, and judged me strongly. Some people who truly cared for me spoke very negatively to me and about me. I did not judge them or their position; I simply had compassion for their opinions, and stayed true to myself. Now, I'm happily married and I enjoy the greatest relationship I could have ever imagined. Not only that, the people who truly cared about me eventually came to embrace my new life and the choices I had made in order to create my new reality.

- Acknowledge the Seasons

This sounds poetic, but it's really very practical. This means you respect that there are seasons in life, and you plan accordingly. One of the biggest mistakes people make is thinking their current conditions are not going to change. This is true in the good times and the bad times.

The majority of people who win the lottery or Powerball jackpots end up broke within a few years.

Why? It's all based on their mindset and belief systems.

They thought the time to reap would never end. Think about how things work on a farm: you plant, you water, and you wait, and you water and you wait, and you fertilize and you wait. Eventually you start to see some growth, and finally some crops. And *then* comes the harvest, where you get the big payout for your efforts.

All good farmers know that the harvest never lasts. So they continue to plan and to save and to plant again. In other words, they are persistent because they know that the seasons of plenty won't last forever.

Life is the same way. However, we have become so accustomed to technology and to having everything right now that we have lost the ability to acknowledge the seasons of our life. We start taking action, we have a few successes, then sometimes we sit back to celebrate and fold our hands a little. There's nothing wrong with taking breaks and enjoying some downtime, as long as we're choosing consciously to do so.

However, if we're not consciously choosing to take a break, then we tend to get complacent.

And then what?

Well, then we lose our momentum and our edge, and our results start to slow down. So we either give up, or we go back to work full blast until we get to a place where we can get comfortable again. What if, instead, we acknowledged that never give up means keeping things going not just in the difficult times, but also in the successful times? It's in those successful times that we need to take advantage of the opportunity to push through to the next level.

On the flipside, acknowledging the seasons means that even when things seem dead and dry, and nothing is happening, we continue to work our plan, even if we don't feel like it.

As I am writing this, we are in the midst of one of the worst recessions in history. Everyone is freaking out. Do you know what a recession is? It's an economic season, and surviving it requires two things: first, that you acknowledge that the seasons of plenty are not going to last and plan accordingly by saving some extra money, and second, that you acknowledge that the time when you are not reaping is the best time to plant seeds.

This means taking action, and understanding that as long as you never give up, the harvest will come again. The same is true in all the dimensions of life, my friend. No matter what is happening, for better or worse, you can eventually have the life that you want, if you Never Give Up.

CHAPTER 8

Dimension #5: Gratitude
Making the Change Worthwhile

Stop right now and let's do an exercise.
Consider these four areas of our lives:

- Health
- Finances
- Career
- Relationships

Now, beginning with your health, start giving thanks for everything that you can think of concerning these four areas of your life. You don't need to know who you are saying thanks to. It can be yourself, it can be God, it can be whatever you believe is responsible for bringing those things into your life.

As you do this, I want you to notice the change in your state. It may not take place instantly, but if you keep at it you will notice a real shift. You may begin to realize that, as you give thanks, the list starts to grow and grow and grow.

This is but a taste of what gratitude can do for you.

Why is gratitude so important to your success?

Well, let me ask you this:

Did you ever do something for someone and feel totally unappreciated?

It might even have been something you were getting paid for, but because the person didn't say "thanks" or "good job," you almost felt that it was for nothing? Most people you talk to value personal praise almost as much as they do financial compensation.

At first this may seem a bit silly. After all, nice words aren't going to pay your bills, are they?

Of course not. But what they do is give you a stronger sense of accomplishment and contribution. You begin to feel that what you are doing is really making a difference. You feel empowered, and you want to keep doing your best. As a recipient of gratitude, you are empowered to become a better person and to give more.

So what happens when you begin to show genuine gratitude toward the people in your life? The more grateful you are, the more you are going to have to be grateful for, because people are going to want to be around you, and to do nice things for you. Gratitude *will* give you more things to be grateful for. It will also inspire other people to be grateful for the things that you do for them.

Gratitude is just one of those things that has a tendency to multiply and take on a life of its own, once it is set in motion. Sometimes all it takes is one person taking the initiative to set things in motion. Then everyone else gets inspired to join in.

Try this in your home or your workplace: give thanks to people and tell them that you appreciate them. See how they respond to you as a result. See how much gratitude and appreciation you get in return. See the way appreciation and gratitude inspire you to give more appreciation, and so on and so on. Try it at your place of work, or try it when you go out and meet people in public.

A lot of the time we get into the mentality that if someone is being paid to do something, we don't need to be thankful. You know how it is: you go through the drive-through or you buy something at the store, and you just drive or walk away without saying anything. You just missed out on a great opportunity to set things in motion and spread some gratitude. As minor as this may seem, it's all a part of the lifestyle you need to build in order to live your dreams.

The habits you build in the little things you do are going to spread to the big things. If you get yourself into the habit of not showing gratitude to people you don't know, it's going to affect the way you interact with the people you do know. If you make it a point to demonstrate genuine appreciation and gratitude for everyone you possibly can, you will notice a shift in your consciousness. You will realize that the level of your gratitude determines the level of your attitude.

But there is another reason gratitude is so important: it changes your focus.

No matter what is going on in your life, there will always be *something* to be thankful for.

Always.

Most people you meet who are really excited and passionate about their lives have as many challenges as the rest of us. But you may hardly be aware of those things.

Why?

Because people who are truly passionate and excited about their lives don't talk about their challenges much, if at all. Instead they deal with them the best they can, and continue to focus their attention on the good things.

In fact, I would be willing to bet that just about anyone who considers themselves to be unlucky or even a failure could change their life just by changing what they choose to focus on.

Does this mean that you deny the bad things in your life?

No, but what it does mean is that you don't give them any more of your attention than you need to, in order to deal with them. Haven't you ever known someone who *always* seems to be unhappy and to have something to complain about? These are the people who consider themselves unfortunate. Even other people may consider them unfortunate.

Most of the time, their lives really aren't as bad as they believe. Not only that, a lot of the things that they are complaining about are things they could fix, if they just started focusing on *changing* them. A strange thing starts to happen when you change the things you focus on. Your attitude about your life starts to change. That attitude affects the way you feel about your life, and you start to value your life more. As you start to value your life more, you start to take action to make it even better. Your actions start bringing you results you can be proud of and grateful for. When you are grateful, the cycle just repeats over and over until you see nothing but good in your life.

As I said before, even the "failures" in your life can be considered positive if you just change your attitude toward them. And the best way to turn around a negative attitude and get yourself pointed in the right direction is with gratitude. You may be starting off your journey "at the end of your rope." But I bet there are at least a dozen things to be grateful for on the list you made at the beginning of this chapter. These might be things that you weren't even thinking of before, that could make all of the difference in your attitude before you even get *any* new results.

The final thing that gratitude will do is to make people *want* to help you. No one wants to do something if they feel unappreciated, that is, unless you are paying them a lot of money to do it. Napoleon Hill said that one of the biggest secrets lucky people know is that when they appear to be lucky more people want to help them. How do you appear lucky?

Well, you focus on the good things that you have in your life and that have happened to you. People will see this, not the bad things that happen to you. They will begin to regard you as a lucky person, and will see that you are thankful for the things you have. They will realize if they help you or support you, you will be grateful to them. Again, gratitude is a self-fulfilling prophecy.

So what are we going to do about this?

Well, we are going to apply something that I call the "gratitude multiplier." This is a process you can begin to use *right now* to attract more good into your life and to surround yourself with people willing to help and believe in you. The point of doing this is to feel good about all the wonderful things in your life. This is not something that you do simply to get what you want out of other people. What you will find, though, is that you will have more people and opportunities to be grateful for in your life. We are going to start with setting yourself on the right foot every single day of your life from now on.

- Give thanks for ten things before you let yourself get out of bed in the morning.

Hey, think about this: it will give you another excuse to hit the snooze button. But seriously, haven't you ever woken up in the morning thinking about something and that one thought set the pace for your entire day? Why not give yourself the best option for having a great day right from the beginning? Sure, you may end up having a rough day anyway, but you might as well get started in the right direction, right off the bat. This is the first step of the gratitude multiplier.

- Show gratitude to *at least* one person you
  know well.

Make it three or even more if you can, but make sure that you show gratitude to *at least* one person per day and make sure that it is someone you know really well. This is important because most of us take the people we know really well for granted *because* we know them well. They are so available to us that we get an entitlement thing going and we forget to show our gratitude toward them. Try this: pretend that something they do for you was done by a total stranger. How thankful would you be then? I don't care how minor it seems: treat it with the respect that it deserves. The best way to do this is to let them know that you are thankful to them for who they are, and not just what they did for you. When you get down to the bottom of it all, this is what people are really after. Sure, it feels nice to know that people appreciate something you have done. But that doesn't even *begin* to compare with knowing that *you* are appreciated.

- Show gratitude to at least one stranger
  every day.

Again, if you can do this for three or more, great. The idea here is to become a person who spreads gratitude everywhere you go. The best way to do that is to get in the habit of being grateful to people you don't know. This is probably the greatest kind of gratitude you can show, because usually you won't be around to enjoy the benefit of it. However, what you will begin to realize is the amazing benefit it has to you when you see your own attitude shift. When it comes to showing gratitude to someone you don't know, the key is being genuine about it. The best way to do this is to let people know *what* you are thanking them for.

For example, you might have someone who serves you at a restaurant. You can say: "thank you for serving us today." This gives them a way to verify that you are not just giving them a canned "thank you" because it is the polite thing to say. It will make the gratitude more genuine to both of you. If you really want to do this right, do it to everyone you can, even the people who don't "deserve" it. Think about it: if you are letting someone else's attitude or behavior affect *your* attitude or behavior toward them, who was the greater force of influence in the situation?

I'm not saying this because you want to be the one in control in every situation. I am saying it so you can begin to gain more control over *your* life, your actions, and your attitude. The more control you have, the better chance you have of getting what you really want.

- Give thanks for ten things right after you go to bed at night.

One of the ways I do this is to utilize goal cards. Every morning and every night I read my goal cards, visualizing each goal as though I've already achieved it. Then, I read an affirmation about how good it feels to have accomplished this specific goal. To create your own powerful goal cards, simply use one 3x5 index card for each of your goals, following this format:

1. At the top of a card, write your specific goal with a date and time deadline.

2. At the bottom of the same card write a corresponding affirmation. An affirmation could be, "I'm enthusiastically enjoying the sunset view from my dream house," or "I'm gratefully and passionately celebrating living at my ideal weight of 185 pounds." Don't worry about perfect grammar; you're looking for an affirmation that strikes an emotion within you.

After you have created a card for each goal, read it, feel it, close your eyes, and visualize it. As you do this, make sure to feel the experience as though you've already accomplished the goal. This will really seal the deal and help you to end the day on a positive note. Again, you might have had a rotten day, but you will *always* have at least ten things to be thankful for. You can be thankful for the fact that you have a bed to sleep in, you can be thankful for the fact that you are literate enough to read this book. You can be thankful that you have food in the refrigerator and that you have clothes to wear and a roof over your head. After all, these things alone make you wealthier than the majority of people in the world.

The secret is to use this gratitude multiplier every single day *for the rest of your life.* When you do, you will find yourself being thankful for more than twenty things per day, and to more than a few people. You'll begin to realize that you truly are a lucky and blessed person. When you do, your whole attitude about life will change, and your life will change along with it. It will also prepare you for the final Dimension of Change.

CHAPTER 9

Dimension #6: Enthusiasm

The Fuel That Keeps Your Engine Burning

Ok, so now we're down to the home stretch.

But before we tackle the final Dimension of Change, let me ask you something: have you ever read a book like this, or listened to a recording, or gone to a seminar, and found that the momentum you had initially experienced just wore off? Maybe you got some results and you were happy with them, but after a while you just got bored and moved on to the next thing.

So what is going to be different this time?

Well, we are going to answer that question in this chapter. As long as you have followed each of the last five Dimensions, this one will come as a fairly natural result. When it does, you'll find that you have the fuel to keep your engine running right on to the finish line and beyond it. But, you may find that there is a bit more to learning how to cultivate *genuine* enthusiasm.

Why?

Because just like all of the other things in this book, enthusiasm is something that will require practice to make it a consistent habit in your life. Most of the time we see people who are enthusiastic and assume that they were just born that way. It looks so natural that they couldn't possibly be faking it. Because we assume enthusiasm comes to them naturally, we don't stop to think that we might be able to *learn* the habit of being enthusiastic.

But do you know what I've found to be true in all circumstances regarding enthusiasm?

I've found that under the right circumstances *anybody* can become genuinely enthusiastic. Some people get jazzed up about cars, some people love sports games, some love concerts or comedy shows, some people get excited at church services, some people love sex (ok, most people), some love power, some even get all worked up over flowcharts and spreadsheets.

The point is that enthusiasm is something *all* of us have at some level, no matter how shy or reserved we may seem about the other things in our lives. In fact, if we hit the right triggers, even the most bottled-up person can bust out of their shell and become genuinely enthusiastic. It's all about getting it touch with your true self, finding your real passion, and getting connected to the universe in a spiritual manner.

So what then?

Do we discover what makes us enthusiastic and just think about it all the time? Well, hold on just a second there, my friend.

First you have to ask yourself this:

What is the point of all this enthusiasm anyway?

Picture this for a second:

A salesperson comes to your door. They are selling cookware, which is something everybody uses. Since you have been thinking about replacing yours anyway, you decide to listen to the sales pitch. They mumble through it in a low, monotone voice, and their face is expressionless. They don't smile, they use very little body language, and after about thirty seconds you find yourself wondering whether you remembered to put your socks in the dryer.

Zzzzzzzz.

How fast would you be ready to go get your checkbook?

Fast! If this guy was selling some coffee to keep you awake! If you are like most people, you are going to politely tell him "no thanks," and go see what kind of cookware sale you can find at a local store.

Now, picture that scenario again. This time the guy is selling you the same thing, but he is so excited about it you just bust out smiling and laughing. Literally, you have never seen someone have so much *fun* talking about cookware. The guy is animated, he's smiling, he's using all kinds of body language, and you start to wonder if maybe he *made* the cookware himself.

Do you think you might be ready to buy something from this guy?

Even if you weren't, you'd probably feel like a million bucks for the rest of the day. Why? Because enthusiasm is like that: it's contagious. It just kind of sticks to you and gets all over you and you can't get it off. Maybe you don't get as worked up as he does about those pots and pans, but you still get a little bit of what he had just by being around him.

Have you ever known someone like that? Of course you have, and you also know how wonderful it is to be in their presence.

Maybe you've been to a seminar and seen someone speak who was full of life, energy, and spunk.

How did you feel after leaving that seminar? I get positive comments and feedback all the time about the keynote speeches and seminars I put on. People love the fire, energy, and passion that I bring to the stage. This is only possible because when I speak I'm in touch with my true self; therefore, my passion and enthusiasm can't help but spill out and have an impact on my audience. Even if my message is something people have heard before in a similar context, I often get a better result based on my delivery method.

While you are thinking about how great you've felt leaving a high-energy and impacting seminar, I want to explain *how* I or another person can create those feelings within you:

That wonderful emotion didn't come from me or another person at all.

It came from *you.*

That's right. Something awoke inside of you that had been there the entire time. You just didn't know it. How else could you walk around for days or even weeks afterward feeling like a million bucks?

But if it truly came from you, why did it eventually wear off?

Enthusiasm is like a spark. You can use it to set off a really big fire, but unless you know how to keep feeding that fire, it burns out. Right now there's a spark inside you just waiting for you to give it the fuel it needs to burn strong and keep burning.

The problem is, as long as you view your enthusiasm as coming from an outside source like a book, recording, or seminar, you keep searching for those kinds of experiences. It's only when you wake up and realize that those things are just throwing gasoline on your fire that you become aware of your personal power to keep it burning. What I am talking about is changing the source of your enthusiasm. I am talking about getting in touch with that little spark inside you and learning to draw on your own source of passion in life.

But before you can do that, let's talk about what enthusiasm actually does. The first thing is what we already mentioned: it inspires other people and it gets that flame burning inside them. But that's not the most important thing that enthusiasm does.

It also blocks out fear and any other kind of negative emotion you might have. Have you ever been so excited about something that you did something really courageous and didn't even realize you were doing it? Maybe it was something so courageous it even seemed stupid to people around you. Did you do it because you were *not* afraid?

Chances are you did it because fear was the furthest thing from your mind.

You weren't even thinking about it, and if you were, it didn't matter. You see, courage is something that comes over you, not in the absence of fear, but in the presence of great passion and enthusiasm. It's when you have a cause to fight for that is bigger than your fear. It makes you conscious of the things that are really important to you, and it helps you to keep your attention focused on that, instead of on all the things that could go wrong.

In fact, most people you meet who live in fear do so because they aren't that jazzed up about where their life is going.

You can spend all your time and energy trying to overcome fear, and it is just going to get worse. Fear is like that: the more attention you give it, the worse it gets. I don't care if that attention is negative, positive, or just a dry analytical approach. Fear feeds on the attention you give it.

But guess what?

So does enthusiasm.

You know, mold can't grow where the sun is shining. In the same way, fear cannot thrive in the presence of great passion. It may still be there, but in order for it to start really messing with your thinking, you have to focus on it and let your enthusiasm take a back seat.

To get clarity about what you want and the way to get it, focus on developing the habits that will get you there: take massive action, fight on in the face of failure, and never give up. Give thanks for all the great things and people in your life every day that you live. Once you have all these factors in place, take hold of that flame inside you, and throw enough gasoline on it to power through any fear directly toward your goals. You will be unstoppable: a force to be reckoned with, and a person who is immune to the influence of fear.

Are you ready?

Ok, let's get started.

First things first:

- Take out the trash

There are things in your life right now that are suffocating your inner fire. Maybe it's the things you are watching on TV, maybe it's someone you know, maybe it's even the kind of music you listen to, or the things you read. No matter what it is, you can't put your foot on the gas and the brake at the same time. Go through your life right now, take inventory of the things that are suffocating your inner fire and passion, and get them out of your life for good.

You only live once. The things in your life that are destroying your potential have no place in the pursuit of your greatest dreams. Think about all the things you could be, do, and have if you just got rid of the junk in your life. Maybe it's the things you have in your house, the people you spend the most time with, the movies you watch, even the things that make you laugh and smile but deliver a message of hopelessness, pain, or negativity. As harmless as those things may seem, you have things you want to do with your future and you must get rid of whatever is preventing you from doing them.

So take out the trash and let's see just how fast we can get this fire burning.

- Find your triggers

Whatever gets you going, let's find a way to get more of it into your life. Yes, eventually you want to be excited and enthusiastic about *everything* in your life, but let's get some sparks going here. Do you love to read a good adventure story or listen to some high-energy rock or some other kind of music? Is there an activity that you love to do or a place you like to go? I don't care how silly it seems, be a kid again and get in touch with something that really makes you come alive. As long as it's not something that is going to distract you from your ultimate goal, find out what lights your fire and find a way to fit it into your life every day. You may not get the chance to go fishing or watch a good hockey game or play a game of golf every single day, but you can read about it, or write about it in a journal.

You can plan your next trip around it, or spend a little time watching a show about it. If there's some-one you know who does it really well, maybe even one of your heroes, get a book about them and start learning about their life. It can be as little as fifteen minutes a day, just as long as it is something that really gets you jazzed up. The key here is to find something that will change your physiology and help you return to a productive state.

• Find your natural "in the zone" state

Ok, this is where we are going to take your natural source of enthusiasm and use it to paint the rest of your life. This means you need to pay attention to the way your body responds to the things you get excited about. You know, you can re-create certain states of mind sometimes just by making changes in your body. For instance, when you are talking about something you are excited about, pay attention to the sound of your voice: the volume, tone, and speed of your speech. All of these things are triggers that your mind will associate with passion and excitement.

Pay attention to the positioning of your body. I bet when you are excited there is a bounce in your step. You hold your head higher, and every motion has life, energy, and certainty. As you begin to notice these things, you get a better idea of the state your entire being is in when you are truly enthusiastic.

Also, pay attention to the state of mind you are in when you are doing what you are passionate about. Are your thoughts directed toward worry or toward hope? What kind of language are you using when you are talking to yourself? Are you talking to yourself the way you would tolerate someone else talking to you? All of these are indications of what state you are in when you are feeling truly alive. You possess the ability to instantly transform into the state where you are productive and feeling good.

And finally:

- Superimpose your state

Now, this is simpler than it sounds. All you have to do is practice it until it becomes a habit. There are two ways that you can do this: the first is to wait until a time when you are doing what you love and take notice of your state: mind, body, emotions, you name it. Once you are solidly focused on this state, picture something you are not terribly sure of that you want to become more confident about. However, instead of focusing on it, picture it like a tiny little pop-up window in the corner of your mind. If your state changes, go back to focusing on what you love and try again. With enough practice you will be able to maintain your enthusiastic state and make that pop-up window bigger and bigger. The idea is to learn to associate your highly enthusiastic state with the other areas of your life.

The other way to superimpose your state is to wait until you are feeling sad or depressed about something you are currently going through. This time, you are going to put the thing you love in your pop-up window. As you "grow" the window out in your mind, adjust your body positioning to match your "in the zone" state. Do this until you have completely blocked out the negative state you were in. Then go back to it. Do this as many times as you have to, until you are able to switch between the states at will.

This is going to take some time, but if you work at it and don't give up, you'll find yourself moving from the consciously ineffective state to the consciously *effective* state, and eventually you will be able to call upon that source of passion at will. Once you are able to do that, you'll have more control over where you focus your energy and your attention. Your mind and body will become trained to follow your focus and you will be able to free your own inner fire from a source that you will always have access to. This will re-condition your mind, and it is extremely effective for consistently impacting the results you get in your life.

You will become the new source of inspiration and passion in your life and in the lives of those around you.

Ok, now you are probably thinking that we are about ready to wrap this up, right?

Well, I can tell you this much: I am not about to leave you without a practical action plan to effectively incorporate these new tools into your life.

Are you ready?

CHAPTER 10

Living Your Dreams
What Most People Never Consider

I want to give you an action plan for really making these things happen, but first we need to talk about the elephant in the room.

Let me start by asking you a question:

How serious are you now about really making these things happen for *yourself?* I mean honestly, how serious are you?

Sure you can read this and watch me jump up and down and get all excited and you can do *everything* that I tell you to do. You can even succeed and still not have what you really want.

You see, my friend, this journey is about more than turning your dreams into reality. It's also about living with those dreams once they *become* reality. It is a journey, but also the most rewarding adventure you will ever embark upon, the journey to your greatest self. This is the greatest journey you will *ever* take. If you are thinking this is easy, then you are doing what most people do:

You are failing to consider that living your dreams is going to be a lifelong commitment. A great dream is not much different than a great relationship: you see someone you really want in your life, you pursue them, and then they become a part of your life.

And then what?

Well, you have two choices: you can either settle down as if the journey is finished, or you can acknowledge that it has just begun. You see, getting what you really want out of life is no guarantee that you will be able to *keep* it, or even enjoy it. You must continue to earn it every day that you live. This is one of the greatest joys of the journey of change, and the thing that makes it all worthwhile.

What I am saying is that earning success is a process, and it is something you are going to be actively involved in for your entire life.

Think about this:

What happens when you earn a paycheck?

Well, anyone who has ever made money knows that it can leave you faster than you have the chance to find out where it is going.

You see, there are a lot of people who don't get what they want because they don't have enough clarity, or they don't develop the right habits. Maybe they don't take action, or they are not grateful for what they have. Maybe they lose their enthusiasm and their drive.

However, I bet that a lot of people also never get what they want because they really have no idea what they would do with it if they *did* get it. Maybe this is why so many people blow extra money when they get it, or waste their weekends until the dreaded Monday morning comes back. We want spare time, but do we know what to do with it when we get it?

We want more money, but do we have a truly meaningful way to use that money that we can be proud of? We want better relationships, but are we willing to pay the price of giving another person the best of who we are?

We want success, but are we willing to deal with all of the adventures, challenges, and even frustrations we might face in keeping it? Do we truly *believe* that we can accomplish everything we desire? Most importantly, do we truly *believe we deserve* these things in life?

Let me make an assumption:

Before you picked up this book, I bet there was at least one thing you could have started doing to make your life better. So why weren't you doing it? Like most of us, you have to at least be willing to ask yourself if you are afraid of what we are all afraid of at some level:

That we are far greater than we even allow ourselves to demonstrate. I can relate to this fear; I have had to do a great amount of work surrounding my self-worth in order to finally believe that I'm capable, talented, and worthy. Don't be afraid! You are great! You can accomplish anything!

Keep in mind…

…there is nothing noble about being poor because we don't believe that money buys happiness. There is nothing noble about being timid or shy because we are afraid of causing envy, inspiring someone, or even shocking people. There is nothing noble about not being excited, passionate, and in love with life, because there is so much suffering in the world.

My friend, the greatest thing that you will ever do for yourself or anyone else is to become everything you were born to be.

Why?

Because it gives other people permission to do the same; it inspires them to follow your example in their own life.

As Marianne Williamson once said, "Your playing small doesn't serve the world. There's nothing enlightened about shrinking so that other people won't feel insecure around you. We were born to manifest the glory of God that is within us. It's not just in some of us, it's in everyone. And as we let our own light shine, we unconsciously give other people the permission to do the same. As we are liberated from our own fear, our presence automatically liberates others."

Yes, it's true that there is a lot of pain in life and there is a lot to be sad, frustrated, or even angry about. But of all the horrible things that happen in this world, there is nothing more tragic than watching someone die on the inside while they are still alive.

This is your life.

It's all out there.

It's waiting for you.

It's *been* waiting for you.

There have always been reasons to let it wait.

There will *always* be reasons.

It's time to stop thinking about those reasons and to get busy.

It's time to wake up and open your eyes to what's going on around you and inside you. It's time to make the decision once and for all that you are going to become the person *you* decide to become, and are meant to become. It's time to let go of all those things that you thought defined you and to focus on what you really want.

Your life depends on it.

What you are going to find out is that even our dreams never turn out just the way we expect them to. That's part of the excitement of making those dreams *real*. There's always a new challenge to meet, another battle to fight, another prize to be won. There's always a reason to take another look at yourself and your life and say, "How can this help me to become an even better person than I am now?" or "How can I use this to inspire people to fight on, when they want to give up?"

No matter how far you may come in this wonderful life…

There's always a reason to keep reaching for more.

There's always a reason to become more than you are.

There's always a reason to never give up.

CHAPTER 11

Living Your Dreams
A Practical Game Plan

Ok, are you ready to start acting on what you've discovered?

What I am going to do now is give you a step-by-step summary and action plan for *using* what you have just finished reading. Now before we do this, let me give you a piece of advice: read this book again. Then read it again and again and again. Read it as many times as you need to, so that you really *get* the premise of the valuable and life changing information that it contains. Why?

Well, because every time you read it you'll get something different out of it. You will be different, and as you re-read the material, it will start to sink into your memory. You will find yourself remembering these things as you are going about your everyday life. It will raise your self-awareness and your confidence, and it will help you to build the habits that will make you successful. I say this not to brag about myself as the writer. Rather, I say this because I know that these principles are true in spite of who teaches them, who learns them, or who ignores them.

So that's your ongoing assignment. Now, let's get moving on this game plan.

Building Consciousness

This step is going to take you at least an afternoon and perhaps an entire day. However, it could literally save you a lifetime of trouble. An entire afternoon is a small price to pay for something that can change the rest of your life. The best thing is that once you have completed this step you will not have to repeat it continuously. However, it may be a good idea to make it a yearly practice. If by any chance you find that one afternoon is not enough, then take two or three. Just be sure not to spend too long on this step, because it can keep you from moving forward. One to three exercises should do the trick for anyone.

Let's get started:

• Identify any "Us and Them" thinking

Ok, hold on, because this is going to get a bit complicated: if you keep thinking in terms of "Us and Them," then you will always be one of "Us," because you feel the way you do about "Them." In other words, if "Them" refers to "rich and snobby" people and "Us" refers to poor and unfortunate people, then you are going to stay poor in order to avoid being seen as "rich and snobby." Most of the time, this works on a subconscious level; people just think they are poor and that there is nothing they can do about it. However, if you view a group of people as being negative, you will never allow yourself to become a part of that group.

Sit down and look at all of the things you want in your life: money, health, success in your relationships, you name it. Then think of the people you know who already have those things. When you start to feel negative patterns or judgments arrive, make note of what they are and where they might have come from. Once you do, the bottom line is you are either going to have to chance that kind of thinking, or get a new goal that can inspire you to become someone you *want* to become. This is about you becoming who *you* want to become, not about trying to be someone else. Take the great behaviors and habits others display, and leave behind the ones that don't "fit" for you.

- Let your imagination go: what would your career, your family, your *life* be like if you could do *anything* you ever set your mind to? By the way, you can!

Really let yourself go on this one, and don't even stop to think about restrictions, no matter how tempted you might be to do so. The object of this exercise is not about setting goals, it's about taking the lid off your thinking. Chances are that you have been limiting yourself for so long that you aren't able to truly consider what you *are* capable of. Allowing yourself to really take the gloves off and dream is going to work wonders for your thinking and help you to start getting in the mindset of *possibility* thinking, instead of limiting yourself to what you think is "reasonable." This feels really good. Block any negativity or doubt that creeps in and just allow yourself to feel what it's like to be grounded and firmly established in your perfect life.

- Assess your untapped potential

Ok, so I can't help you with this one, but that doesn't even matter. I can guarantee that you're using a very limited amount of your true potential. Most of us know where we are pulling punches and selling ourselves short. Take about 30 minutes to write down *all* of the missed opportunities you can think of and all the places where you *know* that you are holding back your talent, your passion, your thinking, and your capacity for action. This is going to give you an idea of what kinds of possibilities await you if you simply up the ante in your life. Don't dwell on missed opportunities; just use them as a reprogramming tool that will allow your mind to recognize your previously untapped potential.

- Acknowledge where you may be wasting energy

This could even mean something you are doing right now. Be honest with yourself about where you might be taking action toward the wrong kinds of things. How do you know if something is wrong? Well, ask yourself if accomplishing it would make your life better, or make you a better person. If not, then chances are you are wasting your energy on something that is keeping you busy but unfulfilled and ineffective. Ask yourself *why* you were unfulfilled and where you may have had expectations that were not met. This is going to show you where you need to cut your losses and focus on what really matters.

- Identify blind spots in your consciousness

Remember that when you numb yourself to your feelings, you numb yourself to *all* of them. Sit down and really take the time to think of the feelings you might have denied or repressed. This means the good and the bad. What you need to start becoming aware of is how you really feel about where your life is going. This will help you to determine what needs to start, and what needs to stop in your life.

• Identify your decoys

This means that you look at the things in your life that have distracted you from your true goals. This is similar to looking at where you might have wasted your energy chasing after things that are really not that important. Now it's time to consider what it has *cost* you to chase after those things. Do you buy things to add more meaning to your life? Do you get involved in addictive or overindulgent behaviors? Whatever it maybe, for better or worse, looking at the consequences will inspire you to make a different choice about how to expend your energy.

• Identify where positive thinking may be your enemy

As I said in the chapter on consciousness, I am all about positive thinking. This is the *only* place where I encourage you to look at the negative. The thing you need to ask yourself is where you are allowing positive thinking to become an excuse to do nothing. Remember, if you are denying that there is a problem, you are never going to work on the solution. Take this time to really reset, and focus on what is working and what is not.

- Assess your awareness of your own timeline

This means that you look at the ways in which you have not been embracing life as it is *right now.* Remember, it is always good to focus on where you want to be in the future. However, if you miss out on your life *now,* then you are likely to miss out on all the rewards you are chasing. This is the first way to look at your timeline. Always remember, your life is happening now.

Next, ask yourself where you have been *too* focused on the here and now, meaning that you are expecting too much too soon, and that you are expecting to have everything *right now*, without giving yourself the chance to develop the habits of patience and persistence. What you need to find out here is how you may be looking at your achievements as a point of arrival, rather than as a process of personal growth. You'll never be completely finished (as long as you're alive anyway), so you might as well enjoy the process. Better to have a long progression of goals that are part of a larger picture than just a string of excuses for chasing after goals for the goals' sake.

- Evaluate your assumptions

These are the areas of your life where you have been accepting things as they are, without stopping to think that they can be changed. It is important not to skip this step. You may be surprised at how many things you just assume are non-negotiable. If there is anything that you are unhappy with, anything at all, question whether it *has* to be that way, or if you can do something about it. I have seen people question things that most people assume "have to be that way." For instance, do you hate the fact that you have to wake up to an alarm clock every morning? What about rush hour traffic? What about the fact that you are living paycheck to paycheck? *All* of these can be changed if you just stop assuming that you are powerless; make a conscious choice right now to take complete control of these things. That is the first step. Once you have done this, ask yourself: "What if I were to change these things today?" Don't worry just yet about how you are going to do it. Most of us are more resourceful than we realize once we decide that we are determined to have something. Think of this as another exercise in overcoming limited thinking.

• Evaluate your habits

Remember the story of the monkey and ask yourself which habits you are still holding on to that either are not working or are no longer relevant in your life. If you are really analytical, you can examine where they came from, but honestly that doesn't make a difference regarding the outcome. All you really need to do is decide that they are out of date, and that they are not going to help you to get what you want. Once you have done this, you can use the exercises later in this chapter to get rid of them.

- Find out what role fear is playing in your life

Fear may be running your life more than you realize, and it's time to call it out from under its rock. Most of the time, fear loses its edge once you confront it. Sit down and identify the thing that you are avoiding the hardest. Ralph Waldo Emerson once said:

"Face the thing you fear most and the death of fear is certain."

This is very true. Realize that where you fear most to act is where you are most likely to have a positive outcome.

Again, there is no point in following this fear to its root or origin. In the end you are left in the same place: confronting it. You may as well cut right to the last step and watch the fear disappear when you take action. To give your confidence a boost in regard to this, think of a time when you confronted fear and it just vanished. If it happened once, it will happen again.

And finally:

- Where am I demanding perfection where it is not possible? What if I shoot for excellence rather than perfection?

Perfectionism is at the root of all fear, and the sooner you let go of being perfect the better off you are going to be. Remember that you may have to let your dream get dinged up in order to make it real. However, that's a better option than clinging to an illusion. Identify where perfection has been your enemy and decide to form the habit of giving yourself room to fail. This will allow you to get moving in areas where you have been stuck for years.

Clarity Step #1 – Getting a Grip on Who You Are

Ok, this is another step that is going to take you a few hours. Like the last one, you only have to do this once or twice, then you will be ready to move on. However, you can also make it a point to do this once a year. Again, the long-term benefits will far outweigh any time that you spend on the exercise.

Let's get started:

- Find your undeveloped areas

This means that you really ask yourself how much of your potential and talent is not being used. You may have to ask some people who know you and who will give it to you straight. Remember, the idea here is that your self-image is not who you are, but who you *believe* you are. It is also the part of you that drives your actions. Find out once and for all where you are selling yourself short and how that relates to your image of what you are capable of, or what you "deserve." As you do this, ask yourself if you have been using any of the following to determine your self-worth:

- Income
- Other people's opinions
- Your appearance
- Performance

Remember: if you are allowing any of these to determine your self-worth, then you need to regain control and base it on who you need to *become* in order to get what you want. Let's be clear, these things are not who you are, and they certainly do not define you.

- Evaluate your needs

Look at your basic emotional needs to determine where you may be either denying yourself or using negative behaviors to meet those needs. This will allow you to replace the pursuit of those needs with positive actions. Look at each of these needs one at a time:

- Security
- Happiness
- Personal Validation
- Love

Once you have these down, you move to the next step in getting clarity:

Clarity Step #2 – Getting a Grip on What You Want

This is the last step before we start to take action. As you do this, you want to look at the results of your exercises on consciousness-building, developing your self-image, and determining what goals you are going to start working on right away. This may require a review of the chapter on clarity. Then write down everything you want for the next year, five years, or even ten years in the following areas to serve as a guide:

- Health
- Finances
- Career
- Relationships

Then move to the four cores of clarity and determine who you need to become to fulfill the roles required to take action and get the results you are after.

- Self-Image
- Roles
- Actions
- Results

Remember, the most important element here is your self-image. This means you must be honest with yourself about who you have to become in order to get where you want to go. And you must contrast that with where you have been. This is why it was so important to find your undeveloped potential. Remember, in regard to clarity it is important to know three things:

- Your destination: who you need to become to get what you want
- Your location: who you are now
- Your map: what habits you will need in order to consistently grow into more of the person you were born to be

These steps may take you several days. That's perfectly fine. Even while you are doing these things, you will notice a change in your actions and attitude. Now it is time to really get focused.

Habits Transformation Plan

Remember that there are four stages involved in transforming your actions:

- Unconsciously ineffective
- Consciously ineffective
- Consciously effective
- Unconsciously effective

The previous exercises should have you well into the third stage. Now you need to develop your plan for getting yourself over the hump. You can get creative about breaking your habits, but make sure you are using the following principles:

- Method Acting
- Interruption
- Replacement

Remember, method acting can be based on more than one person. Just make sure that it is someone who has accomplished what you are after, and that they were able to accomplish it without the rest of their life falling apart.

Interruption can be any of the methods we talked about in the chapter on habit. Just make sure that whatever it is, you are able to stop your old patterns dead in their tracks. Once that is done, replacement will ensure that you don't fall back into the old patterns again.

When it comes to this step, you can look at your needs and find out how your old habits were meeting them. This will help you to develop a habit to replace those ineffective habits, and make sure that your needs are met in a healthy way. Remember, habit transformation is a process, and the more you can make it a part of your everyday life and routine, the better.

Taking Action

Ok, by now you know what you want and have identified all the "junk" that is in your way. Now, take each one of your goals and break them down according to the PLANS method:

- Portions
- Landmarks
- Action
- Negotiation
- Synergy

Steps one and two should take about one hour. Remember, we are not after perfection, because steps three and four are going to help you determine how to refine your plans. As you do this, call your prospective synergy partner and gauge their interest level on holding you accountable. This means that they should be both able and willing to do what you ask. Just make sure this is someone who meets the requirements we talked about in the chapter on action. Please, do yourself a favor and DON'T ask your spouse to do this. Let them decide what their level of involvement will be, and find someone who has more of an outside perspective to get the job done.

Agree to meet with your partner or to email them on a *specific* landmark to keep them updated on your progress. Don't leave this responsibility to them. It's your life. Simply ask them to hold you accountable when you slack off, and to celebrate your successes with you. It can be something as simple as sending a weekly email.

If you are up for it, you can try something I have seen work for a lot of people: have your partner come up with a list of people you love and re-spect, and agree that when you don't meet your goals they will be notified. Yes, this sounds fun-ny, but you would be amazed at how effective it can be. You can also make bets with your partner where you agree to do their laundry or something else really undesirable if you don't stick to your commitment. Get as much leverage on yourself as you can.

Never Give Up – Developing Persistence

This is going to fall under your habit transformation step, but it is the most important habit you can ever form. The best way to develop persistence is to immerse yourself in learning about people who have been persistent themselves, and to follow the steps we covered in the chapter on persistence:

- Get Real – As long as you have followed the previous steps, you should be good here.

- Get Rid of Your Conflicting Agendas – Eliminate your "back up plans."

- Protect Your Dream – How have you allowed others and outside influences to discourage you?

- Acknowledge the Seasons – Keep taking action, in both the good times and the bad.

Persistence is like taking a shower: you have to do it on a regular basis and you will *never* reach a point where you can stop. Take these four areas and make a list that you check yourself on every day. The key is to be consistent: practice persistence until it becomes a habit. For best results, you can use the habit transformation process to develop the habit of persistence.

Applying the Gratitude Multiplier

Much like the cultivation of persistence, gratitude is something you are going to want to make a habit in your life. Begin with asking yourself this question:

- How have I missed the good things in my life by focusing on the negative things?

This can count for both the things you have missed out on because you have taken them for granted and the things you have not had a chance to enjoy. Either way, your level of gratitude is going to determine not only what you receive, but more importantly, how much you get out of what you already have. Once this is done, add the four points of your gratitude multiplier to your daily checklist on persistence.

- Give thanks for ten things before you let yourself get out of bed in the morning.

- Show gratitude to at least one person you know well every day.

- Show gratitude to at least one stranger every day.

- Give thanks for ten things right after you get in bed at night.

Finally, look at the things or the people in your life you have been taking for granted, and get to work on becoming grateful for them. There is a very good chance that many things have come and gone in your life because you have not appreciated them enough. That stops right now. Find the areas where you have let things go and start building up your gratitude toward them. This alone will make a world of difference both in what you receive in your life and in whether or not you keep it.

Building Enthusiasm

This is another habit you are going to be working on for the rest of your life. However, you don't have to worry about doing a lot of extra work and killing yourself every day to develop the habit. Think of it again as taking a shower: you can spend ten minutes a day, or an hour. However, ten minutes is enough.

When it comes to enthusiasm, it would be good to find someone to model, as you did with your habits. No, you don't want to be someone you are not. However, chances are that the person you choose will be someone who is like you in some way. Maybe you see something in them that you *know* exists in you, that you have never been able to truly embrace.

Next, we move to the practice of taking out the trash. You have already done this once, but it is something you want to make a monthly, or even weekly, practice until you get into the habit of guarding yourself against negativity. While you are doing this, set aside one day per week to work on gaining control of your state of mind. Remember the process:

- Find your triggers
- Find your natural "in the zone" state
- Superimpose your state: bad to good and good to bad

Remember that you can do this not only when you are in your good state, but when you are in your bad one. One thing you will want to do is make a habit of stopping yourself as *soon* as you realize that your state is becoming negative. For instance, if you find yourself in a traffic jam at a dead stop, close your eyes and put yourself somewhere else, even if it's just for a second.

What you want to teach yourself in doing this is that you are not *forced* to live in the state you are currently in. You can change it. Sure, it will take work, just like training yourself to lift a heavy weight or run a mile. You can start small and work at it until you build up the emotional muscles you need to take control of your emotional state.

Preparing to Live Your Dreams

Finally, don't underestimate the human tendency to hold on to the way things are, even when they are bad. It's possible that even if you are not happy with where your life is, you are comfortable with it. Realize that most people will remain in unhappiness instead of taking a step into uncertainty. The key to this last step is identifying the things that are going to empower you to live your dreams once they become real. Start by asking yourself this:

• What have I put off, and why?

When you put something off, it's not *just* because of fear. There is *always* some kind of a benefit that you are getting by *not* taking action. Again, lack of action *is* action and it *does* bring results. Find out what kind of results or benefits have been driving you to put off what you have to do. Once you find out what they are, ask yourself if this is more important than having what you really want. Then ask yourself this:

• What are the potential pitfalls of success?

This counts for both the things that are imagined and irrational and the things that are real. When you find out which things are irrational, you can decide to change your focus and to stop giving those things so much credit. On the other hand, you are also going to find that some of the pitfalls are real. Yes, you could argue that there are sacrifices to make in order to get what you want. However, it's not really a sacrifice at all if you're moving your life in the direction you desire. The best way to think of a sacrifice is that you are trading something good for something of greater value. Compare the real pitfalls to what you want, and ask yourself again what is more important. Then ask yourself this:

- What is it going to mean for me and those I love?

Yes, it is your life. However, you still want to consider what the changes in your life are going to mean for your spouse, your children, and everyone else you are close to. This means both in positive and negative ways. The people around you are going to be watching you. They are going to wonder what got into you and why you are making such drastic changes. Some of them are going to be afraid, some of them are going to be ecstatic, and some of them are going to be jealous. However, in the end you are sure to win them all over, as long as you don't give up. The hard part is setting their minds at ease about *why* you are making these changes and where *they* fit into it.

Once you understand the benefits of these changes as they relate to the people who are close to you, you can prepare them, and help win them to your side. Just remember that even if you don't get their support, you will eventually win them over if you ask for support instead of permission. Asking for support means selling people on the benefits the changes will bring to them.

Next, ask yourself this:

- Am I willing to pay the price?

I know that the answer is yes. I believe in you, and you already have everything you need to make these changes happen. However, give yourself one more check before the curtain goes up on the rest of your life. Close your eyes, picture the life that you are after in all of its detail, and live every emotion right now as if it were already yours. Really picture it, take some deep breaths, relax, and allow yourself to feel it as though you were living your perfect life right now, in this moment. As you do this, ask yourself:

"Is it worth it?"

Yes! Yes! Yes!

And finally, ask yourself this:

• How can I give something back to others?

My friend, the book that you hold in your hands is my answer to that question and my gift to you.

Now it is your turn.

We talked about gratitude. This is the best way to it show it for the amazing rewards that await you. I ask nothing in return, aside from the role you are allowing me to play in the rest of your life.

What will you do to pay it forward?

Now go get started.

Your best life is waiting...

CHAPTER 12

Final Words

As we finish up here, I want to tell you how proud I am of you.

The decision to take this massive leap toward your best life takes a lot of courage. The journey of personal development is not a path that many choose, but the treasures which await you are more valuable than any sacrifice you'll make along the way. Just think of where the consistent application of the Six Dimensions of Change will take you in the next year, in five years, and beyond...

I also want to share a personal story of a recent life-changing experience. I had the privilege of becoming a certified Firewalking instructor, and the event was just unbelievable.

I have done a lot of personal performance training, coaching, public speaking, and workshops, but nothing compares with the experience of confronting your fears up close and personal. For four days

I was challenged by event after event to dig even deeper into who I am and what I truly want out of life. I was challenged to overcome the limiting beliefs that still exist within me.

I was fortunate enough to have my wife with me at this event. It was so empowering to have her there because it's tough to explain the level of challenge and excitement that comes from gaining complete control over your emotions and your state of mind. We grew even closer and sharing this experience has deepened our understanding of one another. It is this understanding that strengthens our character; it challenges us to become who we really are.

I would say that the experience was more of a purification process than anything. This is because confronting fear head on is really more about confronting yourself. You know, a goldsmith puts gold over a fire and heats the gold until it becomes liquid. As this happens, the impurities all float to the top and the smith skims them right off. In the same way, the intense moments of life bring you face to face with the flaws and impurities in your own character.

As these things begin to surface, they too can be skimmed off…leaving only pure gold.

This is what you were born to be.

There's tremendous power which becomes yours as you get clarity about who you are, what you want, and what's limiting you. Whether it's firewalking, board breaking, or simply being more assertive in expressing yourself around other people, these are all things which can bring you face-to-face with the limiting beliefs that have taken root inside of you. We're taught so many of these beliefs from the time we're young that we create subconscious pacts with them to protect and rationalize them. But once we confront these fears, we sever our ties with them; they lose their power and evaporate.

It's time my friend.

Time to take control of your life.

It's time to take hold of the prosperity, the love, the passion, the well-being, and all the wonderful things which await you.

I trust that something in this book has spoken to you and that you are beginning to understand the abundance that is all around you, just waiting for you to take hold of it.

As a closing invitation, I would love to have you as a guest at one of my events. Here you'll discover how quickly you can be empowered to transform your life by becoming an active participant in the strategies I teach. Life is a journey, my friend, and I believe you'll come to realize that it's the greatest journey you will ever take. I look forward to the opportunity to meet you and shake your hand.

Until then, learn more, grow more, live more, and become more than you ever imagined.

That's what you've been here for all along.

Enjoy!

For more information about Kenny's coaching services, products, workshops, or to invite him to speak for your organization visit:

www.kennychapman.net.

ABOUT THE AUTHOR

Kenny Chapman is an accredited international speaker and serial entrepreneur. He has owned several different companies in very diverse industries. Kenny is currently the owner of a multi-million dollar service company as well as co-owner of a product-based life improvement business.

Kenny's seminars, books, CD's, and downloadable teachings continue to influence people to become more than they ever thought possible.

Kenny travels extensively for business and pleasure, though the two are usually one and the same. When Kenny's not traveling he enjoys time in western Colorado and southern California with his wife Christy.

For upcoming events, books, audio and video of Kenny, visit his website or call:

877-YOUACHIEVE (877-968-2244)
www.kennychapman.net